Running Room's Training Log

S0-CBM-852

By John Stanton

Personal Information

As the information in this log is vital to its owner, please return if found.

Name _____

Address _____

City _____ Postal/Zip _____

Telephone _____

E-mail address _____

Running Gear Information

Shoes _____ Size _____

T-shirt _____ Size _____

Training shirt _____ Size _____

Shorts _____ Size _____

Tights _____ Size _____

Gloves _____

Hat, cap, toque _____

Personal Records

Distance	Time	Race	Date
5 km			
10 km			
1/2 Marathon			
Marathon			

Running Room's Training Log

...s no such thing as bad weather, just soft people."—Bill Bowerman "Start by doing what's ... then w... possible and suddenly you are doing t... possible."—Saint Francis of A... ...hing ... Only ... th... the ... more associated with success and happines... an any other."—Brian Tracy "Anybody ca... ...ut anything with himself that he really wants to and makes up his mind to do. We are ca... ...ter things than we realize. ... —... "All we need to make us ... appy is something to be enthusiastic ... Charles ... ...u cannot do interfere with what you can do."—John Wooden "... be ... ...not interrupt man doing it."—Ancient Chinese Proverb "Success comes before work ...ictionary."—Anonymous "We should not let our fears hold us back fr... ...ing our hopes."—John F. Kennedy "Conditions are never just right. People who ...on until all factors are favorable do nothing."—William Feather "How to succeed: try ... How to fail: Try too hard."—Malcolm Forbes "There is no failure except in no longer ...lbert Hubbard "I always loved running... it was something you could do by yourself, and u... ...n power. You could go in any direction, fast or slow as you wanted, fighting the wind if you ...eeking out new sights just on the strength of your feet and the courage of your lungs."— ...'Jogging is very beneficial. It's good for your legs and your feet. It's a ...good for the ground. It makes it feel needed."—Charles Schulz, Pea... ...ne who has run knows that its most important value is in removing tension and allowi... ...from whatever other cares the day may bring."—Jimmy Carter "Runners just do it—they ...finish line even if someone else has reached it first."—Anonymous "You have to forget ... ...rathon before you try another. Your mind can't know what's coming."—Frank Shor... ...ll starts with those first basic steps and soon becomes ...nture of a lifetime."—John Stanton "The will to win means nothing if ... the will to prepare."—Juma Ikangaa, 1989 NYC Marathon winner "The greatest pleasu... ...oing what people say you cannot do."—Walter Bagehot "A healthy body is a guest-cha... ...soul; a sick body is a prison."—Francis Bacon "The best way out is always through."—R... ...ost "No army can withstand the strength of an idea whose time has come."—Victor H... ...are clubs you can't belong to, neighborhoods you can't live in, schools you can't get ... ...he roads are always open."—Nike "True sport is always a duel: a duel with nat... ...e's own fear, with one's own fatigue, a duel in which body and mind are strengthened."—Y... ...tushenko, Russian poet "In life, as in football, you won't go far unless you kn... ...the goal posts are."—Arnold Glasgow "Do you really want to get to your g... ...here's a process. It involves one step at a time and it involves patience."—Laurie Skreslet, ...an to climb Mount Everest "We swing ungirded hips, And lighted are our eyes, The rain i... ...We do not run for prize."—Charles Hamilton Sorely, The Song of the Ungirt Runners ... ...portant thing in the Olympic Games is not to win but to take part, just as ...important thing in life is not the triumph but the struggle."—Baro... ...in, founder of the modern Olympic Games, 1890 "To avoid criticism, do nothing, say noth... ...ng."—Elbert Hubbard "The human spirit is indomitable."—Sir Roger Bann... ...n who can drive himself further once the effort gets painful is the man who will win."—Ro... ...er, first 4-minute miler "Happiness lies in good health and a bad memory."—Ingrid Berg... ...improve the present. It is thine."—Henry Longfellow "The Golden Rule is that there ...en rules."—George Bernard Shaw "Compete against yourself, not others."—Jeff Ga... ...on't be afraid to take a big step if one is indicated. You can't cross a chasm in two s... ...—David Lloyd George "We are always getting ready to live, never living."—Ralph Wa... ..."There is no greater glory for a man as long as he lives than th... he wins by his own hands and feet."—Homer "No wind favors him who ...ned port."—Michel de Montaigne "Nothing great was over achieved without enthusiasm ...aldo Emerson "We are not interested in the possibilities of defeat."—Queen Victoria ...st point is my persistence."—Stephen Fekner, runner-manager of the Canadian ultramarat... ...excellence is best measured by the achiever."—Joe Paterno "An hour of f... ...is worth five hours of foot dragging."—Pancho Segura "The last three of four reps is w... ...he muscles grow."—Arnold Schwarzenegger "Ability may get you to the top, but it t...

© 2006, John Stanton
First printed in 2006 5 4 3 2 1
Printed in Canada

All rights reserved. No part of this work covered by the copyrights hereon may be reproduced or used in any form or by any means—graphic, electronic or mechanical—without the prior written permission of the publisher, except for reviewers, who may quote brief passages. Any request for photocopying, recording, taping or storage on information retrieval systems of any part of this work shall be directed in writing to the publisher.

Publisher: Running Room Publishing Inc.
9750 – 47 Ave.
Edmonton, AB T6E 5P3
Canada

Website: www.runningroom.com

Library and Archives Canada Cataloguing in Publication

Stanton, John, 1948-
    Running Room's training log / by John Stanton.

Includes index.
ISBN 0-9739379-6-3

    1. Running. 2. Diaries (Blank-books).
I. Running Room Canada Inc II. Title.

GV1061.5.S82 2006   796.42   C2006-902116-3

Graphic Design: Nancy Gillis
Cover Design: Nancy Gillis

Acknowledgments

This log book is different from a normal book because I have written only half of the book—the second half will be written by you. Over the past 20 years the team at the Running Room has listened to your comments on our training logs and diaries. This log book encapsulates the motivation and inspiration required to keep your training consistent. We listened to your requests to include some of the basic reminders, training schedules and inspirational photos and quotes. You must now supply the perspiration and commitment to see your goals through to fruition. A written account of your daily regimen provides every runner or athlete a clear reflection on their training and documents their progress on the journey of self improvement and excellence in life.

I would like to acknowledge all of the people at the Running Room. Team commitment and passion provided all of the technical support to deliver the log book in a friendly, informative and fun format. I hope you enjoy writing your half of the book in the same way that children enjoy their play.

Stay passionate about running, about people and about having fun!

John Stanton

Table of Contents

Welcome to the *Running Room's Training Log*.

Running is both social and personal. You will receive a special joy along with a real sense of personal reflection about your inner self when you keep a hand-written diary of your running. Some days running provides you with a clarity of thinking and a calmness while other days it is social. Some days a run is just for you the athlete, and it becomes a very individual and personal experience. Other runs are for competition or maybe for completion, while a group run improves your health and wellness and at the same time expands your circle of friends. The solo run works on your self-discipline and courage; the group run allows you to be childlike and think of your running as play.

A log allows you to look at your running as a coach looks at his athlete. By recording your training in a log you can go back days, months and even years to see what worked or what didn't. You can also understand the weather conditions, the course and the duration and intensity of your training. You will look back at your notes to see what comments were made, the weather conditions, who your training buddies were and even how your own training has changed over time. More than anything this log is something you can hold, feel and read—an expression of your innermost goals and aspirations.

We designed this book as a training guide and as a personal diary of your running. In the initial chapters you will find lots of helpful advice, from building your programs to training programs, shoe selection, stretching exercises, information about how to factor in the weather and safety tips. There are some training schedules that provide a tested and proven program for everyone from the beginner to the marathon runner. The diary has lots of room to enter daily training information and 12 months of spaces to record your activity. Each week has a great summary graph to display your week at a glance.

Once you fill in all the information in this log, it truly will become "your book," authored by you, about you and your training. So have fun, train smart and enjoy writing "your book."

Have fun! I look forward to seeing you on the trails and at the races!

Committed to fitness and health,
John Stanton

1 Building
Your Program

The Running Room Training Principles

Stress and Rest

Stress is another word that can be used for training. In brief amounts, exercise or training stress causes a temporary imbalance in the various body processes (muscular, cardiovascular). In response to this imbalance, the body will react by reestablishing equilibrium and will become stronger and more protected from further imbalance. This is called training. After time, the amount of training stress must become greater and greater to establish an imbalance to promote further training.

Rest should always be combined with training stress, as repair and adjustment to the imbalances can only happen when the body is resting. The rest period should be long enough to allow almost complete recovery from the training session but not so long that you lose the training adaptation. When the rest period is too short, or the stress is too great, the body doesn't have time to repair and adjust, which may cause possible fatigue or injury.

Implementing principles of stress and rest into your program will ensure an adequate training stimulus followed by an appropriate rest period. Even in the early stages of a fitness program, physiological balances can be reestablished in approximately 24 hours. Start out by exercising no more than every other day or a minimum of three times per week.

Practicing the principle of stress and rest will also ensure that the training stress is consistent. If a few days of training are missed, the body may lose some tone and endurance. A day or two of hard training will not make up for what was lost. In fact, it may hurt you in the end by causing undue fatigue or injury. The extra physical strain when trying to make up training will do more harm than just tiring you out, so consistency of training is critical for success. The individual who trains consistently will often see greater improvements than one who trains extremely hard at times and skips training at other times. Think of rest as part of every good training program.

Consistency also has its rewards. As proper training continues, an individual will develop a solid fitness base. A solid fitness base will ensure that when interruption to training does occur for a short time, loss of fitness will be minimal.

The stress and rest principle of training is the foundation of any training program. Its purpose is to ensure an appropriate training stress and adequate rest periods, thus resulting in the establishment of a consistent pattern of exercise.

Progressive Overload

Running seems to attract hardworking, goal-oriented people who appreciate the fact that the sport rewards honest effort. These individuals have learned that the more they put in, the more they get out. Running is different. Your willpower and your heart-lung machinery can handle much more work than your musculoskeletal system. Beyond a certain point, it's better to relax about your training than to approach every workout in hyperdrive. The following guidelines show you how you can safely enjoy your running without risking injury.

1. Honestly evaluate your fitness level.

If you haven't had a physical exam lately, have one before you begin your running program. Start out running gently and slow to a walk when you feel tired. Remember: you should be able to carry on a conversation as you run. If you're patient with yourself, you can increase your effort as your body builds strength and adapts to the stress of running.

2. Easy does it.

The generally accepted rule for increasing your distance is to edge upward no more than 10% per week. Beginner runners should add just 1 or 2 km per week to their totals. This doesn't sound like too much, but it will help keep you healthy, and that means you can continue building. Start from a base of 20 km per week; you can build up to 40 km per week (enough to finish a marathon, if that interests you) in 10 to 12 weeks. Your long runs are another consideration. To avoid injury or fatigue, these should be increased by only 2 km per week.

3. Plan for plateaus.

Don't increase your distance every week. Build to a comfortable level and then plateau there to let your body adjust. For example, you might build to 20 km per week and then stay at that training level for three or four weeks before gradually increasing again. Another smart tactic is to scale back periodically. You could build up from 10 to 12 to 14 km per week, and then rest with a 10 km week before moving on to 16 km. Don't allow yourself to get caught up by the thrill of increasing your distance every single week. That simply can't work very long.

4. Make haste slowly.

Another cause of injury and fatigue is increasing the speed of your training runs too much and too often. The same is true of interval workouts, hill running and racing. When the time is right for faster-paced running (after you're completely comfortable with the amount of training you're doing) ease into it just once a week. Never do fast running more than twice a week. Balance your fast workouts and your long runs (both qualify as "hard" days) with slower, shorter days. This is the well-known and widely followed hard-easy system.

5. Strive for efficient running form.

You'll have more fun because you won't be struggling against yourself. Poor running form is the cause of many injuries. For example, running too high on the toes or leaning too far forward can contribute to shin splints and Achilles tendonitis. Carrying the arms too high or swinging the elbows back too far can cause back or shoulder stiffness or injury. To run most efficiently, keep your body straight, and concentrate on lifting your knee just enough to allow your leg to swing forward naturally. Combined with a gentle heel landing, this will give you an economical yet productive stride.

6. Turn away from fad diets; go instead with wholesome foods.

Runners function best on a diet high in complex carbohydrates. That means eating plenty of fruits, vegetables, whole-grain products and low-fat dairy foods and avoiding fried foods, pastries, cookies, ice cream and other fat-laden items. Fish, lean meats and poultry are better for you than their high-fat cousins—sausage, bacon, untrimmed red meats and cold cuts. Generally, you're wise to eat three to four hours before running. That way, you're less likely to experience bloating or nausea. Remember: fluids are vital. Aim to drink 8 to 10 glasses of water a day.

7. Hills place an enormous stress on the cardiovascular system, so it's best to warm up for several miles to raise your heart rate gradually.

When climbing hills, shorten your stride and concentrate on lifting your knees and landing more on the front of your foot. Pump your arms like a cross-country skier. Lean forward but keep your back straight, your hips in, your chest out and your head up. Barreling down a steep hill can multiply skeletal forces several fold, increasing chances of injury. Hold your arms low and tilt your body forward to keep it perpendicular to the slope. Allow your stride to stretch out a little, but don't exaggerate it. Try to avoid the breaking action of landing too hard on your heels.

8. Be smart about injuries.

Runners who interrupt their training programs at the first sign of injury generally recover very quickly. You might not be able to enter the race you're aiming for, but you'll be able to find another one soon. On the other hand, runners who persist in training hard even after they start to break down are courting much more serious injuries. When you develop a persistent running pain, open your eyes and obey the red flag. Stop. Rest. Wait until your body is ready to begin training again. When it is, ease back into your training. Don't try to catch up too quickly: it can't be done.

9. Pay close attention to pain.

It's usually OK to forget mild discomfort if it goes away during a run and doesn't return after. But pain that worsens during a run or that returns after each run cannot be ignored. Remember: pain has a purpose. It's a warning sign from your body that something's wrong. Don't overlook it. Instead, change your running pattern, or if the pain is severe enough, stop running and seek professional help.

"Any Pain, No Brain"

2 Conditioning Programs

Beginner's Conditioning Program

If you are just beginning, start first with walking and add running later. If you have been inactive for a long time, start with a walking program. Walk before you run. Think of it as a preconditioning program.

Start with a fast walk for 20 to 30 minutes. Slow down if you find yourself short of breath. Don't stop. Keep moving. By pumping your arms as you walk and really stepping out, you can increase your heart rate to a level nearly equivalent to a slow run. Also, by walking vigorously uphill, you can add to the rigor of your walking workouts.

Once you can walk briskly for 30 minutes, you can start interspersing some easy running into your walking. By slowly exchanging running for walking, over several weeks you will gradually progress to running for 10 minutes and walking for 1 minute.

The following schedule should be run at least three times per week. All running should be done at a conversation pace, and all walking should be done briskly. Of course, a proper warm-up and cooldown are required. Start and end all sessions with a one-minute walk.

Training Rules

1. This program starts conservatively. You can even fall a little behind and still get back on track easily.

2. Once you reach the halfway mark, you may find it difficult to keep up unless you run faithfully at least three times a week.

3. If you can't keep up or lose time from illness or injury, don't panic—stay at the level you can handle or go back a level until you are ready to move on.

4. Remember, it took you a lot of years to get out of shape; take your time getting back into shape.

Your Goal: The Beginner's Conditioning Program is designed to get you running using the run-walk approach for varying distances (see page 18).

Beginner's Conditioning Program

Week	Training Session	Total Exercise Time	
		Running	**Walking**
1	walk 1 min; run 1 min, walk 2 min x 6 sets; run 1 min, walk 1 min	7 min	14 min
2	walk 1 min; run 1 min, walk 1 min x 10 sets	10 min	11 min
3	walk 1 min; run 2 min, walk 1 min x 6 sets; run 2 min, walk 1 min	14 min	8 min
4	walk 1 min; run 3 min, walk 1 min x 5 sets	15 min	6 min
5	walk 1 min; run 4 min, walk 1 min x 4 sets	16 min	5 min
6	walk 1 min; run 5 min, walk 1 min x 3 sets; run 2 min, walk 1 min	17 min	5 min
7	walk 1 min; run 6 min, walk 1 min x 3 sets	18 min	4 min
8	walk 1 min; run 8 min, walk 1 min x 2 sets; run 2 min, walk 1 min	18 min	4 min
9	walk 1 min; run 10 min, walk 1 min x 2 sets	20 min	3 min
10	walk 1 min; run 10 min, walk 1 min x 2 sets	20 min	3 min

Intermediate Running Conditioning Program

After you can run five minutes nonstop, you are ready for the intermediate program. This phase of training requires that you stay at the level of running for five minutes but do it three to five times a week, for three to four weeks.

Note: When you have reached 30 minutes, three times per week, pause. Hold your running at this level and concentrate on gradually bringing your running time up to 30 minutes on the other days that you are running. You are progressing well, and you don't want to risk injury, fatigue or boredom.

Intermediate Conditioning Program

Week	Training Session	Sessions per Week	Total Exercise Time Running	Walking
1	walk 1 min; run 5 min, walk 1 min x 4 sets	3	20 min	5 min
2	walk 1 min; run 7 min, walk 1 min x 3 sets	3	21 min	4 min
3	walk 1 min; run 10 min, walk 1 min x 2 sets	3	20 min	3 min
4	walk 1 min; run 10 min, walk 1 min x 2 sets	3	20 min	3 min
5	walk 1 min; run 10 min, walk 1 min x 2 sets	3	20 min	3 min
6	walk 1 min; run 10 min, walk 1 min x 2 sets; run 2 min, walk 1 min	3	22 min	4 min
7	walk 1 min; run 10 min, walk 1 min x 2 sets; run 4 min, walk 1 min	3	24 min	4 min
8	walk 1 min; run 10 min, walk 1 min x 2 sets; run 6 min, walk 1 min	3	26 min	4 min
9	walk 1 min; run 10 min, walk 1 min x 2 sets; run 8 min, walk 1 min	3	28 min	4 min
9	walk 1 min; run 10 min, walk 1 min x 2 sets	1	20 min	3 min
10	walk 1 min; run 10 min, walk 1 min x 3 sets	3	30 min	4 min
10	walk 1 min; run 10 min, walk 1 min x 2 sets	1	20 min	3 min

The Advanced 5 K Conditioning Program

If you can currently run 20 minutes or longer on a consistent basis, you are ready for the advanced 5 K program. This program focuses on safely increasing your total running time or distance as well as adding in extra days of training.

After you have reached week 10, when you are running five times a week, hold your longest runs up to 30 minutes and concentrate on gradually bringing your other runs up to 30 minutes as well. You don't want to risk injury, fatigue or boredom.

Advanced Conditioning Program

Week	Training Session	Sessions per Week	Total Exercise Time Running	Walking
1	walk 1 min; run 10 min, walk 1 min x 2 sets	3	20 min	3 min
2	walk 1 min; run 10 min, walk 1 min x 2 sets; run 2 min, walk 1 min	3	22 min	4 min
3	walk 1 min; run 10 min, walk 1 min x 2 sets; run 4 min, walk 1 min	3	24 min	4 min
4	walk 1 min; run 10 min, walk 1 min x 2 sets; run 6 min, walk 1 min	3	26 min	4 min
5	walk 1 min; run 10 min, walk 1 min x 2 sets; run 8 min, walk 1 min	3	28 min	4 min
6	walk 1 min; run 10 min, walk 1 min x 3 sets	3	30 min	4 min
	walk 1 min; run 10 min, walk 1 min x 2 sets	1	20 min	3 min
7	walk 1 min; run 10 min, walk 1 min x 3 sets	3	30 min	4 min
	walk 1 min; run 10 min, walk 1 min x 2 sets; run 2 min, walk 1 min	1	22 min	4 min
8	walk 1 min; run 10 min, walk 1 min x 3 sets; run 3 min, walk 1 min	3	33 min	5 min
	walk 1 min; run 10 min, walk 1 min x 2 sets; run 2 min, walk 1 min	1	22 min	4 min
9	walk 1 min; run 10 min, walk 1 min x 3 sets; run 3 min, walk 1 min	3	33 min	5 min
	walk 1 min; run 10 min, walk 1 min x 2 sets; run 4 min, walk 1 min	1	24 min	4 min
10	walk 1 min; run 10 min, walk 1 min x 3 sets	2	30 min	4 min
	walk 1 min; run 10 min, walk 1 min x 2 sets; run 5 min, walk 1 min	2	25 min	4 min
	walk 1 min; run 10 min, walk 1 min x 2 sets	1	20 min	3 min

3 Running Form

How can I improve my form? This is one of the most frequent questions coaches hear. Before getting into a discussion of form or giving advice to a trainee, I usually suggest that they come with me to the finish area of a local road race, so they can watch the lead runners come in. It is always very apparent that in the lead pack, as in the whole pack, there are some runners with great-looking form and then there are some with butt-ugly form. What I ask the trainee to look at is not the display of form as much as the degree of relaxation. The lead runners are certainly fast, after all they are in the lead at the finish, but if you study their concentration, you can see that they maintain a more relaxed form even under race conditions.

Another thing to do is to go down to a local track area and listen to the advice of the running coach. The number one thing you will hear the coach say during a workout is, "Relax." The coach will be making all kinds of points to the runners, but the basic thing the coach wants the runners to do, no matter how hard they are pushing, is to relax.

So relax, and let's take a look at how to improve your running form.

Posture

Have a buddy videotape your running—both at the start of a run and near the end of a long run. You will end up with a valuable tool to assess any running posture problems. Here are some of the most common problems as well as some tips on how to improve them.

Overstriding

Increase the rhythm of your arm swing and concentrate on shortening your swing. Think of running on hot coals to shorten your reach with each foot stride forward.

Tightness in Shoulders

Learn to relax the palms of your hands by gently touching your thumb to the middle finger. Your fingers should be loose, so make sure you do not grip a fist as you run. Practice running with a couple of soda crackers held in your hands. Cup your hands with your thumbs on top.

Knee Lift

Your knees should be lifted just high enough to clear the ground. Too high a knee lift causes wasted energy—most runners are training for a forward-motion sport.

Arm Carriage

Holding the palms of your hands inward and slightly upward will keep your elbows near your sides. Think of your arm swing being in the general area of your heart. Too high an arm swing results in your heart having to pump uphill. Think of the words "relaxed" and "rhythmic." An increase in your arm swing can help increase the turnover rate of tired legs.

Too Much Bounce

Look at the horizon and concentrate on keeping the head in the same plane. Do some accelerations with an increased body lean. Focus on lower knee lift and try to think of reaching with your arms rather than pumping them.

Perfect Form

There really is no perfect form. Check out the top finishers at some local races: you will see some gazelle-like form alongside some butt-ugly form. The important thing to remember is to stay relaxed, stay rhythmic and push hard. Much of your running form is a gift from your parents, but you can make the most of your gift with some attention to fine tuning your individual form.

Form Tips

1. Stay Upright

Good running posture is simply good body posture. When the head, shoulders and hips are all lined up over the feet, you can move forward as a unit, with a minimum amount of effort.

2. Chest Forward

Many runners let their chest sag into a slouch. In such a position, the lungs won't maximize their efficiency. Before starting your run, relax and take a deep breath, which moves the lungs into an efficient position. After you exhale, maintain the chest in this beneficial alignment. The most efficient way to run is to have your head, neck and shoulders erect.

When you run leaning forward, you're always fighting gravity.

3. Hips Forward

One of the most common errors is letting the hips shift back and the butt stick out behind you. Taking a deep breath often pulls the hips forward and also into an alignment that allows easier running.

4. The Foot Plant

There is a difference between what should happen and what you may be able to control. First, let your shoe professional fit you with a couple of pairs of shoes that are right for you. Then just start running! Your personal stride is the result of your shape, your physique and the strength and balance of your muscles at least all the way up to your waist! Please don't try to change your foot plant as you train: you will not be running naturally and you are very likely to cause more problems than you solve. Changes to your gait only happen as a result of longer-term changes elsewhere. As you gain fitness and strength, you may well notice that many irregularities resolve themselves. Modern training shoes are designed to accommodate biomechanically different feet. Maybe the problem you thought you had will turn out to be not so much of a problem after all. But if you really do have a problem that continues to affect your activity, you may have to seek the advice of a therapist or coach to assess and deal with your particular situation.

5. Arms

Arm position can vary widely from one runner to the next. In general, the arms should swing naturally and loosely from the shoulders. Not too high and not too low. This usually means staying relaxed. Staying relaxed will prevent the arms from being carried too high and too rigid, which will expend more energy than needed. Your hands should never cross the center of your chest. Remember you want your body to go forward and not side-to-side, so your arms should, too. Keep your hands in a relaxed position and try not to clench or make fists.

6. Stride Length

As a coach, my experience has shown that as runners get faster, their stride length shortens. Leg turnover rate, the cadence of the runner's legs, is the key to faster and more efficient running. Staying light on your feet with a more rapid leg turnover rate will keep many of the aches, pains and injuries away, providing injury-free training.

Sprinters have a high knee lift. The long-distance runner, anyone running more than a mile, needs to minimize knee lift. If your knees go too high, you are overusing the quadriceps muscles on the front of the thigh. This overstriding leaves the runner with sore quadriceps at the end of his or her run. Keep your leg turnover light and rapid—more of a shuffle than the sprinter's stride.

Stay relaxed with a low, short stride while lightly touching the ground. This will prevent tightness in the shin, behind the knee or in the back of the thigh in the hamstring. Kicking too far forward tightens up the lower leg and hamstrings.

Do short accelerations while staying light on your feet. Keep your foot strike quieter with each stride, keeping your foot close to the ground to prevent any negative forces of gravity from excessive bounce.

7. Head and Neck

Your torso will normally do what your head is doing. So if you are dropping your head right down, your torso will probably follow and lean too far forward. Keep the neck and shoulders relaxed. Try not to hunch your shoulders, which will cause undue fatigue to that area. Your eyes should be looking somewhere about 20–30 m ahead of you.

8. Practice Your Technique

Once or twice a week, a little technique work is really helpful. After your warm-up, run some accelerations of 50–150 m. Pick one of the elements of good form and feel yourself executing it well during the acceleration. Rehearse each element at least four times, and keep to one or two elements at most in each session. A change in technique may feel a little awkward at first, but you'll know when you've got it right, it feels so good! You can follow the lead of athletes in events like sprinting and hurdling, where effective technique is a vitally important ingredient of success. Their warm-up is actually designed so that their technique (they often call it "skill") is rehearsed every time they prepare for training or competition. Your warm-up consists of a period of jogging and stretching. Build in some technique accelerations, too. They take very little extra time. You'll get the most effective "motor learning" by focusing on one point of technique for a short period of time and repeating it several times. When you're moving your body in a new way, your body gets tired, and quickly! You'll feel it and there will be a noticeable loss in your coordination and motor skill. It's temporary; the short break between accelerations will give you the recovery you need.

4 Proper Shoe Selection

Shoes are a runner's most important piece of equipment. The average runner strikes the ground with a force of 3□ to 5 times their weight, which has to be absorbed by the feet and legs. You have to put some thought into which pair you choose. The right pair of shoes can enhance your performance and prevent injuries.

Proper Shoe Selection

Proper shoe selection is an important part of the prevention of injury. Forces greater than three to five times your body weight are placed on your feet and dissipated up your leg when you run. The right running shoes will accommodate your individual needs and can keep you running comfortably.

Determining Your Foot Type

When you run, after your heel strikes the ground, your foot pronates by rolling inward and flattening out. Your foot then supinates (rotates outward) after the weight is transferred to the ball of your foot. The foot then becomes a rigid lever so that you may propel yourself forward. Perfect running styles are rare. Overpronation is more common than oversupination.

The Overpronator

- Feet roll inward too much when running.
- Generally has low arches.
- Knees and kneecaps move towards the inside of the feet when you bend at the knees.
- More susceptible to runner's knee, iliotibial band syndrome, tendonitis, plantar fasciitis.

The Supinator / Under Pronator

- Lacks normal inward rolling of feet when running.
- Generally has high arches.
- Knees and kneecaps move towards the outside of the feet when you bend at the knees.
- More susceptible to ankle sprains, stress fractures, pain on the outside of the shin and knee, plantar fasciitis.

Reading Old Shoes

Your old shoes reveal many traits about what type of runner you are. If you walk into a Running Room or Walking Room to buy a new pair of running shoes, a salesperson can often put you into the right pair in a matter of moments. Most magicians would never reveal the secrets of their trade, but I can take some of the mystery out of shoe selection with a few tips on how to read your old shoes.

View the upper of the shoe from the rear:

- The shoe's centerline should be perpendicular to the ground.
- The centerline shifts inward, to the medial side of the shoe, if the runner has overpronated.
- The centerline shifts outward, to the lateral side of the shoe, if the runner has supinated.

Check the condition of the midsoles:

- The midsole compresses uniformly if the runner has normal pronation.
- The midsole compresses more on the inside of the shoe if the runner has overpronated.
- The midsole compresses more on the outside of the shoe if the runner has supinated.

Check the wear on the upper:

- The upper retains its shape if the runner has normal pronation.
- The upper sags inward from the toe area if the runner overpronates during push-off.

Shoe Requirements

The Overpronator

- Straight or semicurved last.
- Maximum rear-foot stability.
- Substantial extended medial support.

The Stability

- Semicurved last.

- Moderate pronation control.
- External counters.
- Durable multidensity midsole material.

The Neutral

- Curved or semicurved last.
- Low or moderate rear-foot stability.
- Flexible midsoles.
- Additional cushioning in midsole.

Guidelines to Find the Best Shoe Fit

- Shop in the afternoon to get the right fit.
- Try on both shoes with the same type of sock to be worn during the activity.
- Try on several different models to make a good comparison.
- Walk or jog around the store in the shoes.
- Check the quality of the shoes. Look at the stitching, eyelets and gluing. Feel for bumps inside the shoe.
- The sole should flex only where your foot flexes.
- Your toes should not be pressing against the end of the shoe when standing nor should there be too much room (a centimeter or more). Shoes that are too big or too small can cause injury to the toenails while running.
- The heel counter should fit snugly so that there is no slipping at the heel.
- Shoes should be comfortable on the day you buy them. Don't rely on a break-in period.
- Consult the staff at the Running Room for help in selecting the correct shoe.

Three Types of Shoes

1. Motion Control

You quickly break down midsoles, overpronate and need a firm midsole with a sturdy heel counter.

Motion Control Features

- Straight or semicurved last.
- Maximum rear-foot stability.
- Substantial extended medial support.

2. Cushioning

You need cushioning, a flexible forefoot and no motion control features.

Cushioning Features

- Curved last.
- Low or moderate rear-foot stability.
- Soft midsoles.
- Additional cushioning in midsole.

3. Stability

You need extra cushioning and some degree of stability, and you are not an excessive pronator.

Stability Features

- Semicurved last.
- Moderate pronation control.
- External counters.
- Durable, multidensity midsole materials.

5 How to Stretch

Stretching should be done slowly, without bouncing. Stretch to where you feel a slight, easy stretch (not pain). Hold this feeling for approximately 20 seconds. As you hold the stretch, the feeling of tension should diminish. If it doesn't, ease off slightly into a more comfortable stretch. This easy first stretch readies the tissue for the developmental stretch. After holding the easy stretch, move slightly farther into the stretch until you feel mild tension again. This is the developmental stretch, which should be held for 20 to 30 seconds. This feeling of stretch tension should slightly diminish or stay the same. If the tension increases or becomes painful, you are overstretching. Again, ease off to a comfortable stretch.

The developmental stretch reduces the risk of injuries and will safely increase flexibility. Hold the stretch at a tension that feels comfortable to you. The key to stretching is to keep relaxed while you concentrate on the area to be stretched. Your breathing should be regular. Be sure not to hold your breath. Don't worry how far you can stretch in comparison to others—increased personal flexibility is a guaranteed result of a regular stretching program.

The Stretches

The following are recommended stretches for beginner and novice runners.

Calf

Stand about 3 ft. (1 m) from a wall, railing or tree with your feet flat on the ground, toes slightly turned inward, heels out and back straight. The forward leg should be bent and the rear leg should be gradually straightened until there is tension in the calf. Finally, bend the straight leg at the knee to work closer to the Achilles tendon.

Hamstring

Lie down on your back with one knee bent and foot flat on the ground. Slip a Thera-Band under your other foot, and grab the ends in your hands keeping your knee bent. Slowly straighten this leg. Feel the stretch. Repeat with the other leg.

Quadriceps (also known as "quads")

Place one arm on something handy to balance yourself and use the other hand to pull the foot back when one leg is bent at the knee. The bent knee should touch the other knee. Don't push it forward or pull it back. While this stretch is being executed, the belly button should be pulled up under the rib cage, which is called a pelvic tilt. The tilt protects the back.

Iliotibial Band Stretch

With one leg towards a railing, bench or wall and the other leg slightly bent, cross the leg to be stretched behind the bent leg. Shift your hip towards the wall to stretch the iliotibial band. You should feel the stretch over the hip area.

Buttock Stretch

Sit up straight with one leg straight and the knee of your other leg bent. Place the foot of the bent leg on the outside of the straightened leg. Slowly pull the bent leg towards the opposing shoulder. The buttock of the bent leg will be stretched.

Hip Flexor Stretch

Kneel on one knee and place the other leg forward at a 90-degree stance. Keep the back straight and maintain the pelvic tilt while lunging forward. The rear knee is planted to stretch the hip in front.

6 Weather

Weather and Running

We know that not every day will be a nice fall morning or a brisk spring evening, so we need to prepare. What do you wear? How do you alter your training schedule? How do you protect yourself from the elements? These are some of the issues we will deal with.

Cold-Weather Running Tips

With the temperatures such as they are, keep in mind a few simple rules if you are going out in this weather.

First, if it is -30°C (-22°F) or colder, you do not have to be a hero. Find an alternative to running outside. This could be a great day for cross-training.

1. Wear three layers: base layer, insulating layer and windproof shell. Some clothing is quite efficient, such as Fit-Wear, and if you have this type of clothing then two layers will suffice.

2. Do not expose too much skin. Keep all extremities covered, i.e., ears, hands, wrists, ankles and neck. Your respiratory area (nose and mouth) will stay warm because of the breathing business going on.

3. Apply Bodyglide or another type of body lubricant to any exposed skin to help protect it from the wind and drying effects of the cold.

4. Run in small loops close to your home base. If you find it is getting unbearable, you will not be too far away from shelter.

5. Bring cab fare, cell phone and I.D.

6. Tell someone where you are going (route map) and give that person an idea of your approximate time of arrival.

7. If you start to detect frostbite, seek shelter immediately and warm up. Do not stay out any longer.

Hot-Weather Running

Heat is the one of the endurance athlete's greatest enemies. Heat stress does not need to progress very far before it becomes a medical emergency. It may be unpleasant to contemplate, but heat works on the protein in the body in much the same way as it does on any other protein—it starts to cook! Luckily we have defense mechanisms that protect us. Distance athletes may not like the slowing down that these mechanisms produce, but they are there for our protection. At the first sign of any symptoms, stop, cool off and seek help. Symptoms may include no longer sweating, dizziness, chills and disorientation. Your cooling mechanism operates on water. In hot conditions, you need to drink frequently before, during and after exercise. If you feel thirsty, you are already dehydrated. For the length of normal fitness activities, plain water is your most effective drink. Sports drinks work best immediately after you have finished.

Precautions

There are some precautions you can follow that will make your hot-weather running safer.

1. Drink at least two cups of water before and a cup for every 15 to 20 minutes during your run.

2. Water is the best drink for exercise lasting less than three hours; for exercise over three hours we suggest a sports drink because it will replace lost electrolytes and provide some fuel (sugar) for exercise. If you are going to use a commercial sports drink, be sure to try it in training prior to a race.

3. Wear a vented cap, sun visor, sunglasses and protective sunscreen. If you are sun-sensitive or concerned about sun exposure, wear some of the new long-sleeve CoolMax or Fit-Wear shirts. They are both safe and cool.

4. Lubricate your underarms and inner thighs. Gentlemen, Body-glide your nipples and ladies, the bra line. Doing so will reduce chafing, a common problem in the summer months.

5. Avoid the use of alcoholic beverages. They will only make you feel warmer as their calories are burned quickly, raising your metabolic rate and body temperature. Alcohol is a diuretic, bringing a risk of dehydration.

6. Adjust your intensity to the temperature. In extreme conditions, slow down your pace.

7. Increase your intake of vitamin C. It is a natural and effective defense against heat stroke, cramps, prickly heat rash and exhaustion.

8. Let someone know your route if you are running alone. Better still, run with a buddy—you'll run with less intensity and it will be more social.

9. If you plan to race on a hot-weather holiday, give yourself four to five days to adjust to the heat.

10. Early mornings are the best time to run. Sunset runs can catch you out in the dark.

11. Water running can be very social and a cool, high-quality workout.

12. Include lots of fruit in your diet. Watermelon, oranges, bananas and strawberries are a good way to take in vitamin C and potassium, two nutrients that are lost when we sweat.

13. If you finish your run and you are still outside, take extra clothes with you to avoid being chilled.

14. Savor the odd low-fat frozen treat to reward yourself for keeping the daily workout fun!

15. Skim milk is also a great cool drink. It is very low in fat.

8 Running Safely

Don't Step on the Wild Side

We are always at risk in today's world, but there are a number of things we can do to make our runs safer. Some of these tips will seem strange to people in some areas and all too poignant for others:

- Carry identification. Carry your name and address, a friend or relative's telephone number and your blood type on the inside sole of your running shoe or tied to a lace. Include other relevant medical information.

- Carry thirty-five cents for an emergency telephone call, or carry a cellphone.

- Don't wear jewelry.

- Make sure your friends or relatives know your favorite running routes. Leave the route written down somewhere. If possible, inform someone of which route you are running.

- Run in familiar areas and alter your route pattern. Know the location of telephones, businesses and stores on your route.

- Avoid unpopulated areas, deserted streets and overgrown trails. Especially avoid unlit areas at night. Run clear of parked cars and bushes.

- Stay alert. The more you are aware, the less vulnerable you are.

- Don't wear headphones. Use your hearing to be aware of your surroundings.

- Ignore verbal harassment. Use discretion in acknowledging strangers.

- Look directly at others and be observant. Keep your distance and keep moving.

- Run against traffic, so you can easily see approaching automobiles.

- Wear reflective material if you must run before or after dark.

- Use your intuition about suspicious persons and areas.

- Call the police immediately if something happens to you or if you notice anything out of the ordinary during your run.

- Carry a whistle or noisemaker.

9 Race Day Tips

Rule #1: Relax!

The most important advice we can give to first-time racers is relax. Enjoy yourself. Racing is meant to be a stimulating, memorable experience. It helps the experience to keep things in proper perspective and to use common sense. Even if something goes wrong on your first race—say you get stomach cramps or your shoelaces come untied—it's not the end of the world. You'll live to run and race again.

Race Day Tips for a Great Time

1. Your Goal

Your goal is simply to finish. Your first race is for the experience, not for the competition. Run it knowing your time will be a personal record.

2. Eating and Drinking

On race day, don't eat or drink anything out of the ordinary. This is not the time to experiment, no matter what you may have heard about athletic superfoods. Nor do you have to be concerned with the carbohydrate loading you may have heard is favored by marathon runners. In fact, for your last meal (taken at least three hours before the race start) you might want to eat less than normal, since nervousness could upset your digestive system.

In warm weather, drink 500 ml of water 1 hour before the start, and continue drinking every 10 minutes during the race. You should practice the same on hot-weather training runs. Don't ever forget: heat can kill. Don't try to be a hero in hot races. Adjust your expectations and drink fluids at regular intervals in relationship to the water loss from your perspiration and breathing.

3. Strategy

Planning your race strategy in advance will build your confidence. Break the course into small sections, making sure you know where hills and other key landmarks are located. It's particularly important that you know the last half kilometer of the course. On race day, it's a good idea to warm up by running over the last half kilometer of the course to set a few landmarks in your mind.

4. Getting Ready

When you arrive at the race, don't be intimidated by what you see other runners doing. Many of them are preparing for a hard effort, whereas you want to make sure you save your energy for a more comfortable race. Do some walking, some stretching and some light jogging to loosen up.

5. Lining Up and Starting

Make your way to the back of the starting pack where you won't get caught in the starting sprint. Many marathons have pacing groups; join the group running at the pace you feel comfortable with. Begin slowly. Don't worry about all the runners who take off ahead of you. It's far better to start slowly and catch up later than to begin too fast and be passed by hundreds of runners after a kilometer or two. Once you get room to run freely, move into your normal, relaxed training pace. Maintain that pace (it should be one that allows you to talk comfortably) at least until you reach the halfway mark. Then if you feel strong and want to pick it up, go ahead—but make sure you do it gradually. If you reach a point of struggle, slow down to regather your strength.

6. Walking

Run 10 minutes and walk 1 minute. Nowhere on the entry form does it say that you can't walk. So if you feel the need to, take walking breaks, particularly on the hills. But never stop moving forward unless you are hurt. Disguise your walking breaks by calling them water breaks. Since drinking water is so important during a race, many runners stop and drink when they get to the water tables. You can do the same—getting water plus the rest you need—and no one will be the wiser.

7. Finishing

Keep your pace constant and steady. Don't sprint hard at the finish line. That is not only unwise, but it can be dangerous. Concentrate on finishing with a good, relaxed, strong form.

8. Recovery

After you finish, be sure you walk around for a cooldown. Drink plenty of fluids, especially if it's a hot day. Change into dry clothes as soon as possible, and when you get home, stretch your muscles thoroughly after taking a cool shower. Don't do any running the next day, although it's

OK to swim or bike. You might find it hard to contain your newfound racing enthusiasm, but to run on leg muscles that might be sore would only tempt injury.

10 Training Programs

On the following pages you will find a variety of suggested training schedules. These schedules have been designed to help runners to complete the event and / or to achieve specific time goals. You will see at the bottom of every training schedule a pace chart outlining the pace requirements for each run.

Training Program Workouts

Workouts Long Slow Distance (LSD–Run / Walk)

Long Slow Distance runs are the cornerstone of any distance training program. Take a full minute to walk for every 10 minutes of running. These runs are meant to be done much slower than race pace (60–70% of maximum heart rate), so don't be overly concerned with your pace. These runs work to increase the capillary network in your body and raise your anaerobic threshold. They also mentally prepare you for long races.

A note on LSD Pace

The pace for the long run on the chart includes the walk time. This program provides an upper end (slow) and bottom end (fast) pace to use as a guideline. The upper end pace is preferable because it will keep you injury free. Running at the bottom end pace is a common mistake made by many runners. They try to run at the maximum pace, which is an open invitation to injury. I know of very few runners who have been injured from running too slowly, but loads of runners who incurred injuries by running too fast. In the early stages of the program it is very easy to run the long runs too fast, but like the marathon or half marathon the long runs require discipline and patience. Practice your sense of pace by slowing the long runs down. You will recover faster and remain injury free.

Steady Run

The steady run is a run below targeted race pace (70% maximum heart rate). Run at a comfortable speed; if in doubt, go slowly. The run is broken down into components of running and walking. We encourage you to use the run / walk approach. Walk breaks are a great way to keep you consistent in your training.

Hills

Distance for the day is calculated as the approximate distance covered up and down the hill. Now, you will no doubt have to run to the hill and back from the hill unless of course you drive to the hill. You will need to add your total warm-up and warm-down distance to the totals noted on the training schedule. I recommend a distance of 3 km both ways to ensure adequate warm-up and recovery because hills put a lot of stress on the body. Hills are run at tempo pace (80% maximum heart rate) and must include a heart rate recovery to 120 bpm at the bottom of each hill repeat.

Tempo

Before starting tempo runs include several weeks of hill running to improve your strength, form and confidence. For the tempo runs, run at 80% of your maximum heart rate for 60–80% of your planned race distance to improve your coordination and leg turnover rate. Include a warm-up and cooldown of about three to five minutes. These runs simulate race conditions and the effort required on race day.

Fartlek (Speed Play)

Fartlek runs are spontaneous runs over varying distances and intensity. Run the short bursts at 70–80% of your maximum heart rate, if you are wearing a monitor. Conversation is possible, but you notice increased breathing and heart rate and perspiration. Between these short bursts of hard effort, but no longer than three minutes, add in recovery periods of easy running to bring your heart rate down to 120 beats per minute. Speed play fires up your performance with a burst of speed. The added recovery/rest interval keeps the session attainable and fun.

Walk Adjusted Race Pace

How do we arrive at a "Walk Adjusted" race pace? When you are walking, you are moving slower than your "average run pace." When you are running, you are moving faster than your "average walk pace." The walk adjusted race pace factors in the variation in walking and running speed. The challenge is knowing the average speed of your walking pace. We have devised a formula to calculate moderate walk pace, which allows us to determine the exact splits including running and walking pace. The effect of this calculation is that the "Walk Adjusted" run pace is faster per kilometer than the average race pace. However, when calculated with your walk pace you will end up with your target race pace. You can go on-line at runningroom.com and print out your "Walk Adjusted" pace bands for race day.

Some Important Points

- When you are designing a program to fit your lifestyle, write down the distance or time you plan for a certain day.

- When you race, you may need to adjust your daily and weekly mileage downward to help recovery.

- Never attempt to combine long runs and races on the same day or weekend.

5K Conditioning Program
(Recorded in Minutes)

Week	Sun	Mon	Tue	Wed	Thu	Fri	Sat	Total Time
1	0:25 mins	Off	Off	0:25 mins	Off	0:25 mins	Off	Walk/Run 1:15

Workout: walk 1 min, run 5 min, x4 sets, plus walk 1 min = 25 mins

Week	Sun	Mon	Tue	Wed	Thu	Fri	Sat	Total Time
2	0:25 mins	Off	Off	0:25 mins	Off	0:25 mins	Off	Walk/Run 1:15

Workout: walk 1 min, run 7 min, x3 sets, plus walk 1 min = 25 mins

Week	Sun	Mon	Tue	Wed	Thu	Fri	Sat	Total Time
3	0:23 mins	Off	Off	0:23 mins	Off	0:23 mins	Off	Walk/Run 1:09

Workout: walk 1 min, run 10 min, x2 sets, plus walk 1 min = 23 mins

Week	Sun	Mon	Tue	Wed	Thu	Fri	Sat	Total Time
4	0:23 mins	Off	Off	0:23 mins	Off	0:23 mins	Off	Walk/Run 1:09

Workout: walk 1 min, run 10 min, x2 sets, plus walk 1 min = 23 mins

Week	Sun	Mon	Tue	Wed	Thu	Fri	Sat	Total Time
5	0:26 mins	Off	Off	0:26 mins	Off	0:26 mins	Off	Walk/Run 1:18

Workout: walk 1 min, run 10 min, x2 sets, walk 1 min, run 2 min, plus walk 1 min = 26 mins

Week	Sun	Mon	Tue	Wed	Thu	Fri	Sat	Total Time
6	0:28 mins	Off	Off	0:28 mins	Off	0:28 mins	Off	Walk/Run 1:24

Workout: walk 1 min, run 10 min, x2 sets, walk 1 min, run 4 min, plus walk 1 min = 28 mins

Week	Sun	Mon	Tue	Wed	Thu	Fri	Sat	Total Time
7	0:29 mins	Off	Off	0:29 mins	Off	0:29 mins	Off	Walk/Run 1:27

Workout: walk 1 min, run 10 min, x2 sets, walk 1 min, run 5 min, plus walk 1 min = 29 mins

Week	Sun	Mon	Tue	Wed	Thu	Fri	Sat	Total Time
8	0:30 mins	Off	Off	0:30 mins	Off	0:30 mins	Off	Walk/Run 1:30

Workout: walk 1 min, run 10 min, x2 sets, walk 1 min, run 6 min, plus walk 1 min = 30 mins

Week	Sun	Mon	Tue	Wed	Thu	Fri	Sat	Total Time
9	0:32 mins	Off	Off	0:32 mins	Off	0:32 mins	Off	Walk/Run 1:36

Workout: walk 1 min, run 10 min, x2 sets, walk 1 min, run 8 min, plus walk 1 min = 32 mins

Week	Sun	Mon	Tue	Wed	Thu	Fri	Sat	Total Time
10	0:23 mins	Off	0:34 mins	0:34 mins	Off	0:34 mins	Off	Walk/Run 2:05

Workout: walk 1 min, run 10 min, x2 sets, plus walk 1 min = 23 mins
Workout: walk 1 min, run 10 min, x3 sets, plus walk 1 min = 34 mins

Week	Sun	Mon	Tue	Wed	Thu	Fri	Sat	Total Time
11	Race Day 5K Walk 1/Run 10							Walk/Run 0:30-0:40

Pace Schedule

Don t worry about pace or distance because the goal is to increase the interval of time running/walking.
Week 1 will incorporate 1 min walk/5 min run.
Week 2 will increase to 1 min walk/7 min run.
All other weeks will progress to the formula of 1 min walk/10 min run.

10 K Conditioning Program
(Recorded in Kilometers)

Week	Sun	Mon	Tue	Wed	Thu	Fri	Sat	Total
1	Off	Off	3 Run/Walk	4 Run/Walk	Off	3 Run/Walk	Off	Run/Walk 10
2	5 LSD Run/Walk	Off	3 Run/Walk	4 Run/Walk	Off	3 Run/Walk	Off	Run/Walk 15
3	6 LSD Run/Walk	Off	4 Run/Walk	4 Run/Walk	Off	4 Run/Walk	Off	Run/Walk 18
4	7 LSD Run/Walk	Off	4 Run/Walk	4 Run/Walk	Off	4 Run/Walk	Off	Run/Walk 19
5	8 LSD Run/Walk	Off	3 Run/Walk	3 Hills (400 m hills) 2.5 km	Off	4 Run/Walk	Off	Run/Walk 17.5
6	8 LSD Run/Walk	Off	3 Run/Walk	4 Hills (400 m hills) 3 km	Off	4 Run/Walk	Off	Run/Walk 18
7	8 LSD Run/Walk	Off	3 Run/Walk	5 Hills (400 m hills) 4 km	Off	5 Run/Walk	Off	Run/Walk 20
8	9 LSD Run/Walk	Off	3 Run/Walk	6 Hills (400 m hills) 5 km	Off	5 Run/Walk	Off	Run/Walk 22
9	10 LSD Run/Walk	Off	4 Run/Walk	5 Run/Walk	Off	4 Run/Walk	Off	Run/Walk 23
10	6 LSD Run/Walk	Off	3 Run/Walk	5 Run/Walk	Off	3 Run/Walk	Off	Run/Walk 17
11	10 km Race							Run/Walk 10

Pace Schedule	Don't worry about pace here because the goal is simply to build your training base. Run/Walk Interval = 10 min Running/1 min Walking

Half Marathon To Complete

(Recorded in Kilometers)

Week	Sun	Mon	Tue	Wed	Thu	Fri	Sat	Total
1	Off	Off	Off	3 Steady Run	3 Steady Run	Off	3 Steady Run	9
2	7 LSD Run/Walk	Off	4 Steady Run	3 Steady Run	3 Steady Run	Off	3 Steady Run	20
3	7 LSD Run/Walk	Off	4 Steady Run	3 Steady Run	4 Steady Run	Off	3 Steady Run	21
4	7 LSD Run/Walk	Off	3 Steady Run	4 Steady Run	3 Steady Run	Off	4 Steady Run	21
5	9 LSD Run/Walk	Off	4 Steady Run	3 Steady Run	3 Steady Run	Off	3 Steady Run	22
6	9 LSD Run/Walk	Off	5 Steady Run	3 Steady Run	4 Steady Run	Off	3 Steady Run	24
7	10 LSD Run/Walk	Off	4 Steady Run	3 Hills 2.5 km	5 Steady Run	Off	3 Steady Run	24.5
8	10 LSD Run/Walk	Off	4 Steady Run	4 Hills 3 km	5 Steady Run	Off	4 Steady Run	26
9	12 LSD Run/Walk	Off	4 Steady Run	5 Hills 4 km	6 Steady Run	Off	4 Steady Run	30
10	14 LSD Run/Walk	Off	4 Steady Run	6 Hills 5 km	6 Steady Run	Off	5 Steady Run	34
11	16 LSD Run/Walk	Off	5 Steady Run	7 Hills 5.5 km	7 Steady Run	Off	5 Steady Run	38.5
12	16 LSD Run/Walk	Off	5 Steady Run	8 Hills 6 km	7 Steady Run	Off	6 Steady Run	40
13	12 LSD Run/Walk	Off	5 Steady Run	9 Hills 7 km	8 Steady Run	Off	6 Steady Run	38
14	18 LSD Run/Walk	Off	6 Steady Run	6 Fartlek	8 Steady Run	Off	6 Steady Run	44
15	18 LSD Run/Walk	Off	6 Steady Run	4 Fartlek	8 Steady Run	Off	6 Steady Run	42
16	20 LSD Run/Walk	Off	6 Steady Run	4 Fartlek	8 Steady Run	Off	6 Steady Run	44
17	6 LSD Run/Wak	Off	10 Steady Run	6 Steady Run	Off	Off	3 Steady Run	25
18	Race - Half Marathon							21.1

Pace Schedule	Long Run (LSD)	Steady Run	Tempo/ Fartlek/Hills	Speed	Race	Walk Adjusted Race Pace
To Complete	9:29 10:33	9:29	8:37	7:36	8:32	8:21

Run/Walk Interval = 10 min Running/1 min Walking
Hills are a distance of 400 m

Marathon To Complete
(Recorded in Kilometers)

Week	Sun	Mon	Tue	Wed	Thu	Fri	Sat	Total
1	10 LSD Run/Walk	Off	6 Tempo	10 Tempo	6 Steady Run	Off	6 Steady Run	38
2	10 LSD Run/Walk	Off	6 Tempo	10 Tempo	6 Steady Run	Off	6 Steady Run	38
3	13 LSD Run/Walk	Off	6 Tempo	10 Tempo	8 Steady Run	Off	6 Steady Run	43
4	13 LSD Run/Walk	Off	6 Tempo	10 Tempo	8 Steady Run	Off	6 Steady Run	43
5	16 LSD Run/Walk	Off	6 Tempo	10 Tempo	8 Steady Run	Off	6 Steady Run	46
6	16 LSD Run/Walk	Off	6 Tempo	10 Tempo	8 Steady Run	Off	6 Steady Run	46
7	19 LSD Run/Walk	Off	6 Tempo	4 Hills 5 km	8 Steady Run	Off	6 Steady Run	44
8	23 LSD Run/Walk	Off	6 Tempo	5 Hills 6 km	8 Steady Run	Off	6 Steady Run	49
9	26 LSD Run/Walk	Off	6 Tempo	6 Hills 7 km	8 Steady Run	Off	6 Steady Run	53
10	19 LSD Run/Walk	Off	6 Tempo	7 Hills 8.5 km	8 Steady Run	Off	6 Steady Run	47.5
11	29 LSD Run/Walk	Off	6 Tempo	8 Hills 9.5 km	8 Steady Run	Off	6 Steady Run	58.5
12	29 LSD Run/Walk	Off	6 Tempo	9 Hills 11 km	8 Steady Run	Off	6 Steady Run	60
13	32 LSD Run/Walk	Off	6 Tempo	10 Hills 12 km	8 Steady Run	Off	6 Steady Run	64
14	23 LSD Run/Walk	Off	6 Tempo	10 Fartlek	8 Steady Run	Off	6 Steady Run	53
15	29 LSD Run/Walk	Off	6 Tempo	10 Fartlek	10 Steady Run	Off	6 Steady Run	61
16	32 LSD Run/Walk	Off	6 Tempo	10 Fartlek	10 Steady Run	Off	6 Steady Run	64
17	23 LSD Run/Walk	Off	6 Tempo	10 Fartlek	10 Steady Run	Off	16 Race Pace	65
18	6 Run/Walk	Off	6 Tempo	10 Steady Run	Off	Off	3 Steady Run	25
19	Race - Marathon							42.2

Pace Schedule	Long Run (LSD)	Steady Run	Tempo/ Fartlek/Hills	Speed	Race	Walk Adjusted Race Pace
To Complete	8:37 9:37	8:37	7:48	6:51	7:49	7:36

Run/Walk Interval = 10 min Running/1 min Walking
Hills are a distance of 600 m

Using the Diary

Overview

This training diary was put together to help you record your progress towards your training goals. We've included tips about such things as goal setting, shoe selection, stretching, and safety tips. We have also included tips on starting a training program alone with sample programs from the beginner conditioning program to the marathon training program. These diary pages will help you train and race better. If you track your daily training you are much more likely to remain committed to your training goals and will be better able to identify factors that contribute to overtraining.

Vitals

Tracking your daily vitals will help you identify trends that contribute to possible overtraining and also help you establish a base line for identifying factors that positively influence healthy training. Monitor your resting heart rate and watch for elevations that may indicate fatigue or overtraining. Changes in your weight should always be monitored in order to maintain your ideal weight. Rapid weight loss and/or weight gain should always be a flag to alert you to potential health issues and to alert you to confer with your doctor. Sleep affects us all differently, but we all have a base level of sleep we need to function daily and to maintain a training schedule. Watch for changes in sleep patterns because restless sleep and poor sleep may be another indicator of overtraining.

Recording Heart Rate Information

Resting Heart Rate (RHR)

Heart rate is expressed as beats per minute (bpm). The RHR is a person's heart rate at rest—the lowest number of heartbeats per minute at complete rest. The best time to find out your resting heart rate is in the morning, after a good night's sleep, and before you get out of bed.

On average the heart beats about 60 to 80 times a minute when we're at rest, but for top athletes it can be below 30 bpm. RHR usually rises with age, and it generally decreases as your fitness level increases.

RHR is used to determine one's training Target Heart Rate (THR). Athletes sometimes measure their RHR as one way to find out if they're over trained. An exceptionally high RHR may be a sign of over-exertion or illness.

Average Heart Rate (AHR)

The Average Heart Rate (bpm) figure is a calculation of your average heart rate during your last workout. You can use this measurement to determine the effectiveness of your exercise program and see your progress.

Target Heart Rate (THR)

THR is a range of heart rates that a person chooses to aim for when exercising, based on their personal fitness goals. Target heart rate zones are expressed as percentages of a person's maximum heart rate (MHR). Target heart rate lets you measure your initial fitness level and monitor your progress in a fitness program. For a rough estimate of your maximum heart rate (MHR) subtract your age from 220. For first-time exercisers, have your physician perform a stress test to determine your MHR along with your target zones specific to your goal. This is especially important if you are just starting an exercise program or have not exercised for a prolonged period of time. In our book, *Running Room's Book on Running*, we have an extensive chapter on heart rate training and establishing target heart rate levels.

Why is establishing daily THR so important?

The most effective way to reach your fitness goal is to exercise in your target heart rate zone. There is a target zone that's right for each day's workout. For example, if you want to improve aerobic fitness you need to be working at 70–80% of your MHR, for 40–60 minutes per day, 3 to 4 times per week. Without this information, you would get on a treadmill and not know how hard or how long you should be exercising. In most cases you may be going too easy or too hard. Our friends at Polar Electro (specialist in heart rate monitors) have suggested the following guidelines:

There are three key target zones that will help you achieve specific goals.

60–70%	Lose Weight or Recover
70–80%	Improve Aerobic Fitness
80+ %	Increase Athletic Performance

Improving Overall Fitness

If you have reached a plateau, you should begin to alter the frequency, intensity and duration of your workouts. The body is smart and adapts to routine. If you follow the same program, and have done so for a while, you may have stopped seeing results. Variety is the key. Focus on different workouts, at different target zones, on different days while adjusting your workout time.

Workout Gear

Make notes about the gear you wear because it does affect the quality of your workout. Use this section to track the mileage on your shoes to ensure you are not training on a shoe that has come to the end of its lifecycle. It's important not to train on shoes that have lost their cushioning and support because that will inevitably result in injury. Although we all vary in terms of how long we can train on a pair of shoes, we suggest that shoe be retired from "active training" after 800 km.

Notes

As this is a training diary use this section for personal notes, comments about the workout or to indicate who your training partner was this day. This provides valuable clues to good or bad training and also makes for fun review weeks, months or even years afterwards.

Weekly Summary

We have provided a great little tool here to allow you to see your week at a glance. To create a cumulative bar graph of weekly mileage, apply an appropriate scale at the left margin and simply fill in the bar for each day of training. Some people may want to track mileage while others may want to track total training time.

Graph Samples

Time and Distance Line Graph

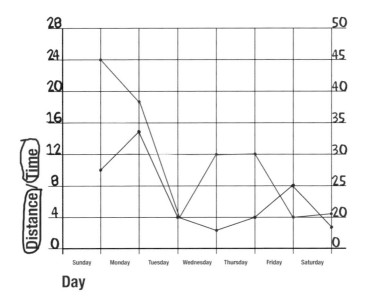

Total Time: 3 hrs 30 min Total Distance: 46.5 K

Time or Distance Bar Graph

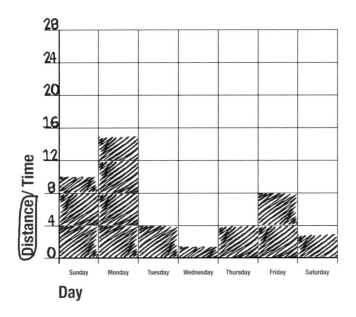

Total Time: 3 hrs 30 min Total Distance: 46.5 K

Vitals:

Resting HR: _____ bpm   Weight: _____ kg/lbs   Hours Slept: _____ hrs

Sport: _____   **Workout:** _____

Course: _____   Duration: _____   Distance: _____

Intensity: ☐ Max. Effort   ☐ Hard Effort   ☐ Medium Effort   ☐ Easy Effort

Average HR: _____ bpm   Target HR: _____ bpm

Feeling: ☐ Fantastic   ☐ Good   ☐ Difficult   ☐ Very Difficult

Weather:

Temperature: _____ ° ___   Workout Gear: _____

Notes: _____

_____

_____

Vitals:

Resting HR: _____ bpm   Weight: _____ kg/lbs   Hours Slept: _____ hrs

Sport: _____   **Workout:** _____

Course: _____   Duration: _____   Distance: _____

Intensity: ☐ Max. Effort   ☐ Hard Effort   ☐ Medium Effort   ☐ Easy Effort

Average HR: _____ bpm   Target HR: _____ bpm

Feeling: ☐ Fantastic   ☐ Good   ☐ Difficult   ☐ Very Difficult

Weather:

Temperature: _____ ° ___   Workout Gear: _____

Notes: _____

_____

_____

Vitals:

Resting HR: _____ bpm   Weight: _____ kg/lbs   Hours Slept: _____ hrs

Sport: _____   **Workout:** _____

Course: _____   Duration: _____   Distance: _____

Intensity: ☐ Max. Effort   ☐ Hard Effort   ☐ Medium Effort   ☐ Easy Effort

Average HR: _____ bpm   Target HR: _____ bpm

Feeling: ☐ Fantastic   ☐ Good   ☐ Difficult   ☐ Very Difficult

Weather:

Temperature: _____ ° ___   Workout Gear: _____

Notes: _____

_____

_____

Vitals:

Resting HR: _____ bpm   Weight: _____ kg/lbs   Hours Slept: _____ hrs

Sport: _____   **Workout:** _____

Course: _____   Duration: _____   Distance: _____

Intensity: ☐ Max. Effort   ☐ Hard Effort   ☐ Medium Effort   ☐ Easy Effort

Average HR: _____ bpm   Target HR: _____ bpm

Feeling: ☐ Fantastic   ☐ Good   ☐ Difficult   ☐ Very Difficult

Weather:

Temperature: _____ ° ___   Workout Gear: _____

Notes: _____

_____

_____

Thursday

Vitals:

Resting HR: _____ bpm   Weight: _____ kg/lbs   Hours Slept: _____ hrs

Sport: _____   **Workout:** _____

Course: _____   Duration: _____   Distance: _____

Intensity: ☐ Max. Effort   ☐ Hard Effort   ☐ Medium Effort   ☐ Easy Effort

Average HR: _____ bpm   Target HR: _____ bpm

Feeling: ☐ Fantastic   ☐ Good   ☐ Difficult   ☐ Very Difficult

Weather:

Temperature: _____ ° ___   Workout Gear: _____

Notes: _____

_____

_____

Friday

Vitals:

Resting HR: _____ bpm   Weight: _____ kg/lbs   Hours Slept: _____ hrs

Sport: _____   **Workout:** _____

Course: _____   Duration: _____   Distance: _____

Intensity: ☐ Max. Effort   ☐ Hard Effort   ☐ Medium Effort   ☐ Easy Effort

Average HR: _____ bpm   Target HR: _____ bpm

Feeling: ☐ Fantastic   ☐ Good   ☐ Difficult   ☐ Very Difficult

Weather:

Temperature: _____ ° ___   Workout Gear: _____

Notes: _____

_____

_____

Vitals:

Resting HR: _____ bpm   Weight: _____ kg/lbs   Hours Slept: _____ hrs

Sport: _____   **Workout:** _____

Course: _____   Duration: _____   Distance: _____

Intensity: ☐ Max. Effort   ☐ Hard Effort   ☐ Medium Effort   ☐ Easy Effort

Average HR: _____ bpm   Target HR: _____ bpm

Feeling: ☐ Fantastic   ☐ Good   ☐ Difficult   ☐ Very Difficult

Weather:

Temperature: _____ ° ___   Workout Gear: _____

Notes: _____

_____

_____

Week Summary

Day

Total Time: _____ Total Distance: _____

Additional Notes: _____

_____

_____

_____

_____

_____

"Start by doing
what's necessary,
then what's possible
and suddenly you are
doing the impossible."
— Saint Francis of Assisi

Vitals:

Resting HR: _____ bpm   Weight: _____ kg/lbs   Hours Slept: _____ hrs

Sport: _____   **Workout:** _____

Course: _____   Duration: _____   Distance: _____

Intensity: □ Max. Effort   □ Hard Effort   □ Medium Effort   □ Easy Effort

Average HR: _____ bpm   Target HR: _____ bpm

Feeling: □ Fantastic   □ Good   □ Difficult   □ Very Difficult

Weather:

Temperature: _____ ° ___   Workout Gear: _____

Notes: _____

_____

_____

Vitals:

Resting HR: _____ bpm   Weight: _____ kg/lbs   Hours Slept: _____ hrs

Sport: _____   **Workout:** _____

Course: _____   Duration: _____   Distance: _____

Intensity: □ Max. Effort   □ Hard Effort   □ Medium Effort   □ Easy Effort

Average HR: _____ bpm   Target HR: _____ bpm

Feeling: □ Fantastic   □ Good   □ Difficult   □ Very Difficult

Weather:

Temperature: _____ ° ___   Workout Gear: _____

Notes: _____

_____

_____

Vitals:

Resting HR: _____ bpm   Weight: _____ kg/lbs   Hours Slept: _____ hrs

Sport: _____   **Workout:** _____

Course: _____   Duration: _____   Distance: _____

Intensity: □ Max. Effort   □ Hard Effort   □ Medium Effort   □ Easy Effort

Average HR: _____ bpm   Target HR: _____ bpm

Feeling: □ Fantastic   □ Good   □ Difficult   □ Very Difficult

Weather:

Temperature: _____ ° ___   Workout Gear: _____

Notes: _____

_____

_____

Wednesday Week 2

Vitals:

Resting HR: _____ bpm   Weight: _____ kg/lbs   Hours Slept: _____ hrs

Sport: _____   **Workout:** _____

Course: _____   Duration: _____   Distance: _____

Intensity: ☐ Max. Effort   ☐ Hard Effort   ☐ Medium Effort   ☐ Easy Effort

Average HR: _____ bpm   Target HR: _____ bpm

Feeling: ☐ Fantastic   ☐ Good   ☐ Difficult   ☐ Very Difficult

Weather:

Temperature: _____ ° ___   Workout Gear: _____

Notes: _____
_____
_____

Thursday

Vitals:

Resting HR: _____ bpm   Weight: _____ kg/lbs   Hours Slept: _____ hrs

Sport: _____   **Workout:** _____

Course: _____   Duration: _____   Distance: _____

Intensity: ☐ Max. Effort   ☐ Hard Effort   ☐ Medium Effort   ☐ Easy Effort

Average HR: _____ bpm   Target HR: _____ bpm

Feeling: ☐ Fantastic   ☐ Good   ☐ Difficult   ☐ Very Difficult

Weather:

Temperature: _____ ° ___   Workout Gear: _____

Notes: _____
_____
_____

Friday

Vitals:

Resting HR: _____ bpm   Weight: _____ kg/lbs   Hours Slept: _____ hrs

Sport: _____   **Workout:** _____

Course: _____   Duration: _____   Distance: _____

Intensity: ☐ Max. Effort   ☐ Hard Effort   ☐ Medium Effort   ☐ Easy Effort

Average HR: _____ bpm   Target HR: _____ bpm

Feeling: ☐ Fantastic   ☐ Good   ☐ Difficult   ☐ Very Difficult

Weather:

Temperature: _____ ° ___   Workout Gear: _____

Notes: _____
_____
_____

Week 2 — Date: ▯ ▯ ▯ — Saturday

Vitals:

Resting HR: _____ bpm   Weight: _____ kg/lbs   Hours Slept: _____ hrs

Sport: _____   **Workout:** _____

Course: _____   Duration: _____   Distance: _____

Intensity: ☐ Max. Effort   ☐ Hard Effort   ☐ Medium Effort   ☐ Easy Effort

Average HR: _____ bpm   Target HR: _____ bpm

Feeling: ☐ Fantastic   ☐ Good   ☐ Difficult   ☐ Very Difficult

Weather:

Temperature: _____ ° ___   Workout Gear: _____

Notes: _____
_____
_____

Week Summary

Total Time: _____ Total Distance: _____

Additional Notes: _____
_____
_____
_____
_____

66

Vitals:

Resting HR: _____ bpm   Weight: _____ kg/lbs   Hours Slept: _____ hrs

Sport: _____   **Workout:** _____

Course: _____   Duration: _____   Distance: _____

Intensity: ☐ Max. Effort   ☐ Hard Effort   ☐ Medium Effort   ☐ Easy Effort

Average HR: _____ bpm   Target HR: _____ bpm

Feeling: ☐ Fantastic   ☐ Good   ☐ Difficult   ☐ Very Difficult

Weather:

Temperature: _____ ° ___   Workout Gear: _____

Notes: _____

_____

_____

Monday

Vitals:

Resting HR: _____ bpm   Weight: _____ kg/lbs   Hours Slept: _____ hrs

Sport: _____   **Workout:** _____

Course: _____   Duration: _____   Distance: _____

Intensity: ☐ Max. Effort   ☐ Hard Effort   ☐ Medium Effort   ☐ Easy Effort

Average HR: _____ bpm   Target HR: _____ bpm

Feeling: ☐ Fantastic   ☐ Good   ☐ Difficult   ☐ Very Difficult

Weather:

Temperature: _____ ° ___   Workout Gear: _____

Notes: _____

_____

_____

Tuesday

Vitals:

Resting HR: _____ bpm   Weight: _____ kg/lbs   Hours Slept: _____ hrs

Sport: _____   **Workout:** _____

Course: _____   Duration: _____   Distance: _____

Intensity: ☐ Max. Effort   ☐ Hard Effort   ☐ Medium Effort   ☐ Easy Effort

Average HR: _____ bpm   Target HR: _____ bpm

Feeling: ☐ Fantastic   ☐ Good   ☐ Difficult   ☐ Very Difficult

Weather:

Temperature: _____ ° ___   Workout Gear: _____

Notes: _____

_____

_____

Wednesday Week 3

Vitals:
Resting HR: _____ bpm   Weight: _____ kg/lbs   Hours Slept: _____ hrs

Sport: _____   **Workout:** _____
Course: _____   Duration: _____   Distance: _____
Intensity: □ Max. Effort   □ Hard Effort   □ Medium Effort   □ Easy Effort
Average HR: _____ bpm   Target HR: _____ bpm
Feeling: □ Fantastic   □ Good   □ Difficult   □ Very Difficult

Weather:
Temperature: _____ ° ___   Workout Gear: _____

Notes: _____
_____
_____

Thursday

Vitals:
Resting HR: _____ bpm   Weight: _____ kg/lbs   Hours Slept: _____ hrs

Sport: _____   **Workout:** _____
Course: _____   Duration: _____   Distance: _____
Intensity: □ Max. Effort   □ Hard Effort   □ Medium Effort   □ Easy Effort
Average HR: _____ bpm   Target HR: _____ bpm
Feeling: □ Fantastic   □ Good   □ Difficult   □ Very Difficult

Weather:
Temperature: _____ ° ___   Workout Gear: _____

Notes: _____
_____
_____

Friday

Vitals:
Resting HR: _____ bpm   Weight: _____ kg/lbs   Hours Slept: _____ hrs

Sport: _____   **Workout:** _____
Course: _____   Duration: _____   Distance: _____
Intensity: □ Max. Effort   □ Hard Effort   □ Medium Effort   □ Easy Effort
Average HR: _____ bpm   Target HR: _____ bpm
Feeling: □ Fantastic   □ Good   □ Difficult   □ Very Difficult

Weather:
Temperature: _____ ° ___   Workout Gear: _____

Notes: _____
_____
_____

Vitals:

Resting HR: _____ bpm   Weight: _____ kg/lbs   Hours Slept: _____ hrs

Sport: _____   Workout: _____

Course: _____   Duration: _____   Distance: _____

Intensity: ☐ Max. Effort   ☐ Hard Effort   ☐ Medium Effort   ☐ Easy Effort

Average HR: _____ bpm   Target HR: _____ bpm

Feeling: ☐ Fantastic   ☐ Good   ☐ Difficult   ☐ Very Difficult

Weather:

Temperature: _____ ° ___   Workout Gear: _____

Notes: _____

_____

_____

Week Summary

Distance / Time (y-axis)

Sunday   Monday   Tuesday   Wednesday   Thursday   Friday   Saturday

Day

Total Time: _____ Total Distance: _____

Additional Notes: _____

_____

_____

_____

_____

_____

"No army can withstand the strength of an idea whose time has come." —Victor Hugo

Vitals:

Resting HR: _____ bpm   Weight: _____ kg/lbs   Hours Slept: _____ hrs

Sport: _____   **Workout:** _____

Course: _____   Duration: _____   Distance: _____

Intensity: ☐ Max. Effort ☐ Hard Effort ☐ Medium Effort ☐ Easy Effort

Average HR: _____ bpm   Target HR: _____ bpm

Feeling: ☐ Fantastic ☐ Good ☐ Difficult ☐ Very Difficult

Weather:

Temperature: _____ ° ___   Workout Gear: _____

Notes: _____
_____
_____

Vitals:

Resting HR: _____ bpm   Weight: _____ kg/lbs   Hours Slept: _____ hrs

Sport: _____   **Workout:** _____

Course: _____   Duration: _____   Distance: _____

Intensity: ☐ Max. Effort ☐ Hard Effort ☐ Medium Effort ☐ Easy Effort

Average HR: _____ bpm   Target HR: _____ bpm

Feeling: ☐ Fantastic ☐ Good ☐ Difficult ☐ Very Difficult

Weather:

Temperature: _____ ° ___   Workout Gear: _____

Notes: _____
_____
_____

Vitals:

Resting HR: _____ bpm   Weight: _____ kg/lbs   Hours Slept: _____ hrs

Sport: _____   **Workout:** _____

Course: _____   Duration: _____   Distance: _____

Intensity: ☐ Max. Effort ☐ Hard Effort ☐ Medium Effort ☐ Easy Effort

Average HR: _____ bpm   Target HR: _____ bpm

Feeling: ☐ Fantastic ☐ Good ☐ Difficult ☐ Very Difficult

Weather:

Temperature: _____ ° ___   Workout Gear: _____

Notes: _____
_____
_____

Wednesday   Week 4

Vitals:

Resting HR: _____ bpm   Weight: _____ kg/lbs   Hours Slept: _____ hrs

Sport: _____ **Workout:** _____

Course: _____   Duration: _____   Distance: _____

Intensity: ☐ Max. Effort ☐ Hard Effort   ☐ Medium Effort   ☐ Easy Effort

Average HR: _____ bpm   Target HR: _____ bpm

Feeling: ☐ Fantastic   ☐ Good   ☐ Difficult   ☐ Very Difficult

Weather:

Temperature: _____ ° ___   Workout Gear: _____

Notes: _____
_____
_____

Thursday

Vitals:

Resting HR: _____ bpm   Weight: _____ kg/lbs   Hours Slept: _____ hrs

Sport: _____ **Workout:** _____

Course: _____   Duration: _____   Distance: _____

Intensity: ☐ Max. Effort ☐ Hard Effort   ☐ Medium Effort   ☐ Easy Effort

Average HR: _____ bpm   Target HR: _____ bpm

Feeling: ☐ Fantastic   ☐ Good   ☐ Difficult   ☐ Very Difficult

Weather:

Temperature: _____ ° ___   Workout Gear: _____

Notes: _____
_____
_____

Friday

Vitals:

Resting HR: _____ bpm   Weight: ___ _ kg/lbs   Hours Slept: _____ hrs

Sport: _____ **Workout:** _____

Course: _____   Duration: _____   Distance: _____

Intensity: ☐ Max. Effort ☐ Hard Effort   ☐ Medium Effort   ☐ Easy Effort

Average HR: _____ bpm   Target HR: _____ bpm

Feeling: ☐ Fantastic   ☐ Good   ☐ Difficult   ☐ Very Difficult

Weather:

Temperature: _____ ° ___   Workout Gear: _____

Notes: _____
_____
_____

Week 4   Date: ☐ ☐ ☐   Saturday

Vitals:
Resting HR: _____ bpm   Weight: _____ kg/lbs   Hours Slept: _____ hrs

Sport: _____   Workout: _____

Course: _____   Duration: _____   Distance: _____

Intensity: ☐ Max. Effort   ☐ Hard Effort   ☐ Medium Effort   ☐ Easy Effort

Average HR: _____ bpm   Target HR: _____ bpm

Feeling: ☐ Fantastic   ☐ Good   ☐ Difficult   ☐ Very Difficult

Weather:
Temperature: _____ ° ___   Workout Gear: _____

Notes: _____
_____
_____

Week Summary

Total Time: _____ Total Distance: _____

Additional Notes: _____
_____
_____
_____
_____

74

"Success comes before work only in the dictionary."
— Anonymous

Vitals:

Resting HR: _____ bpm   Weight: _____ kg/lbs   Hours Slept: _____ hrs

Sport: _____   **Workout:** _____

Course: _____   Duration: _____   Distance: _____

Intensity: ☐ Max. Effort   ☐ Hard Effort   ☐ Medium Effort   ☐ Easy Effort

Average HR: _____ bpm   Target HR: _____ bpm

Feeling: ☐ Fantastic   ☐ Good   ☐ Difficult   ☐ Very Difficult

Weather:

Temperature: _____°____   Workout Gear: _____

Notes: _____

_____

_____

Monday

Vitals:

Resting HR: _____ bpm   Weight: _____ kg/lbs   Hours Slept: _____ hrs

Sport: _____   **Workout:** _____

Course: _____   Duration: _____   Distance: _____

Intensity: ☐ Max. Effort   ☐ Hard Effort   ☐ Medium Effort   ☐ Easy Effort

Average HR: _____ bpm   Target HR: _____ bpm

Feeling: ☐ Fantastic   ☐ Good   ☐ Difficult   ☐ Very Difficult

Weather:

Temperature: _____°____   Workout Gear: _____

Notes: _____

_____

_____

Tuesday

Vitals:

Resting HR: _____ bpm   Weight: _____ kg/lbs   Hours Slept: _____ hrs

Sport: _____   **Workout:** _____

Course: _____   Duration: _____   Distance: _____

Intensity: ☐ Max. Effort   ☐ Hard Effort   ☐ Medium Effort   ☐ Easy Effort

Average HR: _____ bpm   Target HR: _____ bpm

Feeling: ☐ Fantastic   ☐ Good   ☐ Difficult   ☐ Very Difficult

Weather:

Temperature: _____°____   Workout Gear: _____

Notes: _____

_____

_____

Vitals:

Resting HR: _____ bpm   Weight: _____ kg/lbs   Hours Slept: _____ hrs

Sport: _____   **Workout:** _____

Course: _____   Duration: _____   Distance: _____

Intensity: ☐ Max. Effort   ☐ Hard Effort   ☐ Medium Effort   ☐ Easy Effort

Average HR: _____ bpm   Target HR: _____ bpm

Feeling: ☐ Fantastic   ☐ Good   ☐ Difficult   ☐ Very Difficult

Weather:

Temperature: _____°____   Workout Gear: _____

Notes: _____

_____

_____

Thursday

Vitals:

Resting HR: _____ bpm   Weight: _____ kg/lbs   Hours Slept: _____ hrs

Sport: _____   **Workout:** _____

Course: _____   Duration: _____   Distance: _____

Intensity: ☐ Max. Effort   ☐ Hard Effort   ☐ Medium Effort   ☐ Easy Effort

Average HR: _____ bpm   Target HR: _____ bpm

Feeling: ☐ Fantastic   ☐ Good   ☐ Difficult   ☐ Very Difficult

Weather:

Temperature: _____°____   Workout Gear: _____

Notes: _____

_____

_____

Friday

Vitals:

Resting HR: _____ bpm   Weight: _____ kg/lbs   Hours Slept: _____ hrs

Sport: _____   **Workout:** _____

Course: _____   Duration: _____   Distance: _____

Intensity: ☐ Max. Effort   ☐ Hard Effort   ☐ Medium Effort   ☐ Easy Effort

Average HR: _____ bpm   Target HR: _____ bpm

Feeling: ☐ Fantastic   ☐ Good   ☐ Difficult   ☐ Very Difficult

Weather:

Temperature: _____°____   Workout Gear: _____

Notes: _____

_____

_____

Vitals:

Resting HR: _____ bpm   Weight: _____ kg/lbs   Hours Slept: _____ hrs

Sport: _____ Workout: _____

Course: _____   Duration: _____   Distance: _____

Intensity: ☐ Max. Effort   ☐ Hard Effort   ☐ Medium Effort   ☐ Easy Effort

Average HR: _____ bpm   Target HR: _____ bpm

Feeling: ☐ Fantastic   ☐ Good   ☐ Difficult   ☐ Very Difficult

Weather:

Temperature: _____°___   Workout Gear: _____

Notes: _____
_____
_____

Week Summary

Distance / Time

| | Sunday | Monday | Tuesday | Wednesday | Thursday | Friday | Saturday |

Day

Total Time: _____ Total Distance: _____

Additional Notes: _____
_____
_____
_____
_____
_____

"Treat each day as a new challenge,
say to yourself that you can
accomplish or achieve any intelligent
goal that you set forth
for yourself."

— John Stanton

Vitals:

Resting HR: _____ bpm　　Weight: _____ kg/lbs　Hours Slept: _____ hrs

Sport: _____　**Workout:** _____

Course: _____　　Duration: _____　　Distance: _____

Intensity:　☐ Max. Effort　☐ Hard Effort　☐ Medium Effort　☐ Easy Effort

Average HR: _____ bpm　　Target HR: _____ bpm

Feeling:　☐ Fantastic　☐ Good　☐ Difficult　☐ Very Difficult

Weather:

Temperature: _____ ° ___　　Workout Gear: _____

Notes: _____

_____

_____

Vitals:

Resting HR: _____ bpm　　Weight: _____ kg/lbs　Hours Slept: _____ hrs

Sport: _____　**Workout:** _____

Course: _____　　Duration: _____　　Distance: _____

Intensity:　☐ Max. Effort　☐ Hard Effort　☐ Medium Effort　☐ Easy Effort

Average HR: _____ bpm　　Target HR: _____ bpm

Feeling:　☐ Fantastic　☐ Good　☐ Difficult　☐ Very Difficult

Weather:

Temperature: _____ ° ___　　Workout Gear: _____

Notes: _____

_____

_____

Vitals:

Resting HR: _____ bpm　　Weight: _____ ' kg/lbs　Hours Slept: _____ hrs

Sport: _____　**Workout:** _____

Course: _____　　Duration: _____　　Distance: _____

Intensity:　☐ Max. Effort　☐ Hard Effort　☐ Medium Effort　☐ Easy Effort

Average HR: _____ bpm　　Target HR: _____ bpm

Feeling:　☐ Fantastic　☐ Good　☐ Difficult　☐ Very Difficult

Weather:

Temperature: _____ ° ___　　Workout Gear: _____

Notes: _____

_____

_____

Vitals:

Resting HR: _____ bpm   Weight: _____ kg/lbs   Hours Slept: _____ hrs

Sport: _____   Workout: _____

Course: _____   Duration: _____   Distance: _____

Intensity: ☐ Max. Effort   ☐ Hard Effort   ☐ Medium Effort   ☐ Easy Effort

Average HR: _____ bpm   Target HR: _____ bpm

Feeling: ☐ Fantastic   ☐ Good   ☐ Difficult   ☐ Very Difficult

Weather:

Temperature: _____ ° ___   Workout Gear: _____

Notes: _____

_____

_____

Thursday

Vitals:

Resting HR: _____ bpm   Weight: _____ kg/lbs   Hours Slept: _____ hrs

Sport: _____   Workout: _____

Course: _____   Duration: _____   Distance: _____

Intensity: ☐ Max. Effort   ☐ Hard Effort   ☐ Medium Effort   ☐ Easy Effort

Average HR: _____ bpm   Target HR: _____ bpm

Feeling: ☐ Fantastic   ☐ Good   ☐ Difficult   ☐ Very Difficult

Weather:

Temperature: _____ ° ___   Workout Gear: _____

Notes: _____

_____

_____

Friday

Vitals:

Resting HR: _____ bpm   Weight: _____ kg/lbs   Hours Slept: _____ hrs

Sport: _____   Workout: _____

Course: _____   Duration: _____   Distance: _____

Intensity: ☐ Max. Effort   ☐ Hard Effort   ☐ Medium Effort   ☐ Easy Effort

Average HR: _____ bpm   Target HR: _____ bpm

Feeling: ☐ Fantastic   ☐ Good   ☐ Difficult   ☐ Very Difficult

Weather:

Temperature: _____ ° ___   Workout Gear: _____

Notes: _____

_____

_____

Vitals:

Resting HR: _____ bpm   Weight: _____ kg/lbs   Hours Slept: _____ hrs

Sport: _____   **Workout:** _____

Course: _____   Duration: _____   Distance: _____

Intensity: ☐ Max. Effort   ☐ Hard Effort   ☐ Medium Effort   ☐ Easy Effort

Average HR: _____ bpm   Target HR: _____ bpm

Feeling: ☐ Fantastic   ☐ Good   ☐ Difficult   ☐ Very Difficult

Weather:

Temperature: _____ ° ___   Workout Gear: _____

Notes: _____

_____

_____

Week Summary

Total Time: _____   Total Distance: _____

Additional Notes: _____

_____

_____

_____

_____

_____

"Hills are speedwork in disguise."

— Frank Shorter

Vitals:

Resting HR: _____ bpm   Weight: _____ kg/lbs   Hours Slept: _____ hrs

Sport: _____   **Workout:** _____

Course: _____   Duration: _____   Distance: _____

Intensity: ☐ Max. Effort   ☐ Hard Effort   ☐ Medium Effort   ☐ Easy Effort

Average HR: _____ bpm   Target HR: _____ bpm

Feeling: ☐ Fantastic   ☐ Good   ☐ Difficult   ☐ Very Difficult

Weather:

Temperature: _____ ° ___   Workout Gear: _____

Notes: _____

_____

_____

Vitals:

Resting HR: _____ bpm   Weight: _____ kg/lbs   Hours Slept: _____ hrs

Sport: _____   **Workout:** _____

Course: _____   Duration: _____   Distance: _____

Intensity: ☐ Max. Effort   ☐ Hard Effort   ☐ Medium Effort   ☐ Easy Effort

Average HR: _____ bpm   Target HR: _____ bpm

Feeling: ☐ Fantastic   ☐ Good   ☐ Difficult   ☐ Very Difficult

Weather:

Temperature: _____ ° ___   Workout Gear: _____

Notes: _____

_____

_____

Vitals:

Resting HR: _____ bpm   Weight: _____ kg/lbs   Hours Slept: _____ hrs

Sport: _____   **Workout:** _____

Course: _____   Duration: _____   Distance: _____

Intensity: ☐ Max. Effort   ☐ Hard Effort   ☐ Medium Effort   ☐ Easy Effort

Average HR: _____ bpm   Target HR: _____ bpm

Feeling: ☐ Fantastic   ☐ Good   ☐ Difficult   ☐ Very Difficult

Weather:

Temperature: _____ ° ___   Workout Gear: _____

Notes: _____

_____

_____

Vitals:

Resting HR: _____ bpm   Weight: _____ kg/lbs   Hours Slept: _____ hrs

Sport: _____   **Workout:** _____

Course: _____   Duration: _____   Distance: _____

Intensity: ☐ Max. Effort   ☐ Hard Effort   ☐ Medium Effort   ☐ Easy Effort

Average HR: _____ bpm   Target HR: _____ bpm

Feeling: ☐ Fantastic   ☐ Good   ☐ Difficult   ☐ Very Difficult

Weather:

Temperature: _____ ° ___   Workout Gear: _____

Notes: _____

_____

_____

Thursday

Vitals:

Resting HR: _____ bpm   Weight: _____ kg/lbs   Hours Slept: _____ hrs

Sport: _____   **Workout:** _____

Course: _____   Duration: _____   Distance: _____

Intensity: ☐ Max. Effort   ☐ Hard Effort   ☐ Medium Effort   ☐ Easy Effort

Average HR: _____ bpm   Target HR: _____ bpm

Feeling: ☐ Fantastic   ☐ Good   ☐ Difficult   ☐ Very Difficult

Weather:

Temperature: _____ ° ___   Workout Gear: _____

Notes: _____

_____

_____

Friday

Vitals:

Resting HR: _____ bpm   Weight: _____ kg/lbs   Hours Slept: _____ hrs

Sport: _____   **Workout:** _____

Course: _____   Duration: _____   Distance: _____

Intensity: ☐ Max. Effort   ☐ Hard Effort   ☐ Medium Effort   ☐ Easy Effort

Average HR: _____ bpm   Target HR: _____ bpm

Feeling: ☐ Fantastic   ☐ Good   ☐ Difficult   ☐ Very Difficult

Weather:

Temperature: _____ ° ___   Workout Gear: _____

Notes: _____

_____

_____

Vitals:

Resting HR: _____ bpm   Weight: _____ kg/lbs   Hours Slept: _____ hrs

Sport: _____   Workout: _____

Course: _____   Duration: _____   Distance: _____

Intensity: ☐ Max. Effort   ☐ Hard Effort   ☐ Medium Effort   ☐ Easy Effort

Average HR: _____ bpm   Target HR: _____ bpm

Feeling: ☐ Fantastic   ☐ Good   ☐ Difficult   ☐ Very Difficult

Weather:

Temperature: _____ ° ___   Workout Gear: _____

Notes: _____

_____

_____

Week Summary

Total Time: _____   Total Distance: _____

Additional Notes: _____

_____

_____

_____

_____

_____

"Stadiums are for spectators. We runners have nature and that is much better."

— Juha "the" Cruel Väätätainen

Vitals:

Resting HR: _____ bpm   Weight: _____ kg/lbs   Hours Slept: _____ hrs

Sport: _____   **Workout:** _____

Course: _____   Duration: _____   Distance: _____

Intensity: ▢ Max. Effort   ▢ Hard Effort   ▢ Medium Effort   ▢ Easy Effort

Average HR: _____ bpm   Target HR: _____ bpm

Feeling: ▢ Fantastic   ▢ Good   ▢ Difficult   ▢ Very Difficult

Weather:

Temperature: _____ ° ___   Workout Gear: _____

Notes: _____

_____

_____

Vitals:

Resting HR: _____ bpm   Weight: _____ kg/lbs   Hours Slept: _____ hrs

Sport: _____   **Workout:** _____

Course: _____   Duration: _____   Distance: _____

Intensity: ▢ Max. Effort   ▢ Hard Effort   ▢ Medium Effort   ▢ Easy Effort

Average HR: _____ bpm   Target HR: _____ bpm

Feeling: ▢ Fantastic   ▢ Good   ▢ Difficult   ▢ Very Difficult

Weather:

Temperature: _____ ° ___   Workout Gear: _____

Notes: _____

_____

_____

Vitals:

Resting HR: _____ bpm   Weight: _____ kg/lbs   Hours Slept: _____ hrs

Sport: _____   **Workout:** _____

Course: _____   Duration: _____   Distance: _____

Intensity: ▢ Max. Effort   ▢ Hard Effort   ▢ Medium Effort   ▢ Easy Effort

Average HR: _____ bpm   Target HR: _____ bpm

Feeling: ▢ Fantastic   ▢ Good   ▢ Difficult   ▢ Very Difficult

Weather:

Temperature: _____ ° ___   Workout Gear: _____

Notes: _____

_____

_____

Vitals:

Resting HR: _____ bpm   Weight: _____ kg/lbs   Hours Slept: _____ hrs

Sport: _____   **Workout:** _____

Course: _____   Duration: _____   Distance: _____

Intensity: ☐ Max. Effort   ☐ Hard Effort   ☐ Medium Effort   ☐ Easy Effort

Average HR: _____ bpm   Target HR: _____ bpm

Feeling: ☐ Fantastic   ☐ Good   ☐ Difficult   ☐ Very Difficult

Weather:

Temperature: _____°___   Workout Gear: _____

Notes: _____
_____
_____

Thursday

Vitals:

Resting HR: _____ bpm   Weight: _____ kg/lbs   Hours Slept: _____ hrs

Sport: _____   **Workout:** _____

Course: _____   Duration: _____   Distance: _____

Intensity: ☐ Max. Effort   ☐ Hard Effort   ☐ Medium Effort   ☐ Easy Effort

Average HR: _____ bpm   Target HR: _____ bpm

Feeling: ☐ Fantastic   ☐ Good   ☐ Difficult   ☐ Very Difficult

Weather:

Temperature: _____°___   Workout Gear: _____

Notes: _____
_____
_____

Friday

Vitals:

Resting HR: _____ bpm   Weight: _____ kg/lbs   Hours Slept: _____ hrs

Sport: _____   **Workout:** _____

Course: _____   Duration: _____   Distance: _____

Intensity: ☐ Max. Effort   ☐ Hard Effort   ☐ Medium Effort   ☐ Easy Effort

Average HR: _____ bpm   Target HR: _____ bpm

Feeling: ☐ Fantastic   ☐ Good   ☐ Difficult   ☐ Very Difficult

Weather:

Temperature: _____°___   Workout Gear: _____

Notes: _____
_____
_____

Vitals:

Resting HR: _____ bpm   Weight: _____ kg/lbs   Hours Slept: _____ hrs

Sport: _____   Workout: _____

Course: _____   Duration: _____   Distance: _____

Intensity: ☐ Max. Effort   ☐ Hard Effort   ☐ Medium Effort   ☐ Easy Effort

Average HR: _____ bpm   Target HR: _____ bpm

Feeling: ☐ Fantastic   ☐ Good   ☐ Difficult   ☐ Very Difficult

Weather:

Temperature: _____ ° ___   Workout Gear: _____

Notes: _____

_____

_____

Week Summary

Distance / Time

Sunday   Monday   Tuesday   Wednesday   Thursday   Friday   Saturday

Day

Total Time: _____ Total Distance: _____

Additional Notes: _____

_____

_____

_____

_____

_____

"Conditions are never just right. People who delay action until all factors are favorable do nothing."
— William Feather

Vitals:

Resting HR: _____ bpm   Weight: _____ kg/lbs   Hours Slept: _____ hrs

Sport: _____   **Workout:** _____

Course: _____   Duration: _____   Distance: _____

Intensity: ☐ Max. Effort   ☐ Hard Effort   ☐ Medium Effort   ☐ Easy Effort

Average HR: _____ bpm   Target HR: _____ bpm

Feeling: ☐ Fantastic   ☐ Good   ☐ Difficult   ☐ Very Difficult

Weather:

Temperature: _____°___   Workout Gear: _____

Notes: _____

_____

_____

Monday

Vitals:

Resting HR: _____ bpm   Weight: _____ kg/lbs   Hours Slept: _____ hrs

Sport: _____   **Workout:** _____

Course: _____   Duration: _____   Distance: _____

Intensity: ☐ Max. Effort   ☐ Hard Effort   ☐ Medium Effort   ☐ Easy Effort

Average HR: _____ bpm   Target HR: _____ bpm

Feeling: ☐ Fantastic   ☐ Good   ☐ Difficult   ☐ Very Difficult

Weather:

Temperature: _____°___   Workout Gear: _____

Notes: _____

_____

_____

Tuesday

Vitals:

Resting HR: _____ bpm   Weight: _____ kg/lbs   Hours Slept: _____ hrs

Sport: _____   **Workout:** _____

Course: _____   Duration: _____   Distance: _____

Intensity: ☐ Max. Effort   ☐ Hard Effort   ☐ Medium Effort   ☐ Easy Effort

Average HR: _____ bpm   Target HR: _____ bpm

Feeling: ☐ Fantastic   ☐ Good   ☐ Difficult   ☐ Very Difficult

Weather:

Temperature: _____°___   Workout Gear: _____

Notes: _____

_____

_____

Vitals:

Resting HR: _____ bpm   Weight: _____ kg/lbs   Hours Slept: _____ hrs

Sport: _____   **Workout:** _____

Course: _____   Duration: _____   Distance: _____

Intensity: ☐ Max. Effort   ☐ Hard Effort   ☐ Medium Effort   ☐ Easy Effort

Average HR: _____ bpm   Target HR: _____ bpm

Feeling: ☐ Fantastic   ☐ Good   ☐ Difficult   ☐ Very Difficult

Weather:

Temperature: _____ ° ___   Workout Gear: _____

Notes: _____

_____

_____

Thursday

Vitals:

Resting HR: _____ bpm   Weight: _____ kg/lbs   Hours Slept: _____ hrs

Sport: _____   **Workout:** _____

Course: _____   Duration: _____   Distance: _____

Intensity: ☐ Max. Effort   ☐ Hard Effort   ☐ Medium Effort   ☐ Easy Effort

Average HR: _____ bpm   Target HR: _____ bpm

Feeling: ☐ Fantastic   ☐ Good   ☐ Difficult   ☐ Very Difficult

Weather:

Temperature: _____ ° ___   Workout Gear: _____

Notes: _____

_____

_____

Friday

Vitals:

Resting HR: _____ bpm   Weight: _____ kg/lbs   Hours Slept: _____ hrs

Sport: _____   **Workout:** _____

Course: _____   Duration: _____   Distance: _____

Intensity: ☐ Max. Effort   ☐ Hard Effort   ☐ Medium Effort   ☐ Easy Effort

Average HR: _____ bpm   Target HR: _____ bpm

Feeling: ☐ Fantastic   ☐ Good   ☐ Difficult   ☐ Very Difficult

Weather:

Temperature: _____ ° ___   Workout Gear: _____

Notes: _____

_____

_____

Vitals:

Resting HR: _____ bpm   Weight: _____ kg/lbs   Hours Slept: _____ hrs

Sport: _____   **Workout:** _____

Course: _____   Duration: _____   Distance: _____

Intensity: ☐ Max. Effort   ☐ Hard Effort   ☐ Medium Effort   ☐ Easy Effort

Average HR: _____ bpm   Target HR: _____ bpm

Feeling: ☐ Fantastic   ☐ Good   ☐ Difficult   ☐ Very Difficult

Weather:

Temperature: _____ ° ___   Workout Gear: _____

Notes: _____
_____
_____

Week Summary

Distance / Time

Sunday   Monday   Tuesday   Wednesday   Thursday   Friday   Saturday

· **Day**

Total Time: _____ Total Distance: _____

Additional Notes: _____
_____
_____
_____
_____

"YOU HAVE TO FORGET YOUR LAST MARATHON BEFORE YOU TRY ANOTHER. YOUR MIND CAN'T KNOW WHAT'S COMING."

— FRANK SHORTER

Vitals:

Resting HR: _____ bpm   Weight: _____ kg/lbs   Hours Slept: _____ hrs

Sport: _____   **Workout:** _____

Course: _____   Duration: _____   Distance: _____

Intensity: ☐ Max. Effort   ☐ Hard Effort   ☐ Medium Effort   ☐ Easy Effort

Average HR: _____ bpm   Target HR: _____ bpm

Feeling: ☐ Fantastic   ☐ Good   ☐ Difficult   ☐ Very Difficult

Weather:

Temperature: _____ ° ___   Workout Gear: _____

Notes: _____
_____
_____

Monday

Vitals:

Resting HR: _____ bpm   Weight: _____ kg/lbs   Hours Slept: _____ hrs

Sport: _____   **Workout:** _____

Course: _____   Duration: _____   Distance: _____

Intensity: ☐ Max. Effort   ☐ Hard Effort   ☐ Medium Effort   ☐ Easy Effort

Average HR: _____ bpm   Target HR: _____ bpm

Feeling: ☐ Fantastic   ☐ Good   ☐ Difficult   ☐ Very Difficult

Weather:

Temperature: _____ ° ___   Workout Gear: _____

Notes: _____
_____
_____

Tuesday

Vitals:

Resting HR: _____ bpm   Weight: _____ kg/lbs   Hours Slept: _____ hrs

Sport: _____   **Workout:** _____

Course: _____   Duration: _____   Distance: _____

Intensity: ☐ Max. Effort   ☐ Hard Effort   ☐ Medium Effort   ☐ Easy Effort

Average HR: _____ bpm   Target HR: _____ bpm

Feeling: ☐ Fantastic   ☐ Good   ☐ Difficult   ☐ Very Difficult

Weather:

Temperature: _____ ° ___   Workout Gear: _____

Notes: _____
_____
_____

Wednesday Week 10

Vitals:

Resting HR: _____ bpm   Weight: _____ kg/lbs   Hours Slept: _____ hrs

Sport: _____   **Workout:** _____

Course: _____   Duration: _____   Distance: _____

Intensity: ☐ Max. Effort   ☐ Hard Effort   ☐ Medium Effort   ☐ Easy Effort

Average HR: _____ bpm   Target HR: _____ bpm

Feeling: ☐ Fantastic   ☐ Good   ☐ Difficult   ☐ Very Difficult

Weather:

Temperature: _____ ° ___   Workout Gear: _____

Notes: _____
_____
_____

Thursday

Vitals:

Resting HR: _____ bpm   Weight: _____ kg/lbs   Hours Slept: _____ hrs

Sport: _____   **Workout:** _____

Course: _____   Duration: _____   Distance: _____

Intensity: ☐ Max. Effort   ☐ Hard Effort   ☐ Medium Effort   ☐ Easy Effort

Average HR: _____ bpm   Target HR: _____ bpm

Feeling: ☐ Fantastic   ☐ Good   ☐ Difficult   ☐ Very Difficult

Weather:

Temperature: _____ ° ___   Workout Gear: _____

Notes: _____
_____
_____

Friday

Vitals:

Resting HR: _____ bpm   Weight: _____ kg/lbs   Hours Slept: _____ hrs

Sport: _____   **Workout:** _____

Course: _____   Duration: _____   Distance: _____

Intensity: ☐ Max. Effort   ☐ Hard Effort   ☐ Medium Effort   ☐ Easy Effort

Average HR: _____ bpm   Target HR: _____ bpm

Feeling: ☐ Fantastic   ☐ Good   ☐ Difficult   ☐ Very Difficult

Weather:

Temperature: _____ ° ___   Workout Gear: _____

Notes: _____
_____
_____

Vitals:

Resting HR: _____ bpm   Weight: _____ kg/lbs   Hours Slept: _____ hrs

Sport: _____   **Workout:** _____

Course: _____   Duration: _____   Distance: _____

Intensity: ☐ Max. Effort   ☐ Hard Effort   ☐ Medium Effort   ☐ Easy Effort

Average HR: _____ bpm   Target HR: _____ bpm

Feeling: ☐ Fantastic   ☐ Good   ☐ Difficult   ☐ Very Difficult

Weather:

Temperature: _____ ° ___   Workout Gear: _____

Notes: _____

_____

_____

Week Summary

Day

Total Time: _____ Total Distance: _____

Additional Notes: _____

_____

_____

_____

_____

Vitals:

Resting HR: _____ bpm   Weight: _____ kg/lbs   Hours Slept: _____ hrs

Sport: _____   Workout: _____

Course: _____   Duration: _____   Distance: _____

Intensity: ☐ Max. Effort   ☐ Hard Effort   ☐ Medium Effort   ☐ Easy Effort

Average HR: _____ bpm   Target HR: _____ bpm

Feeling: ☐ Fantastic   ☐ Good   ☐ Difficult   ☐ Very Difficult

Weather:

Temperature: _____ ° ___   Workout Gear: _____

Notes: _____

_____

_____

Vitals:

Resting HR: _____ bpm   Weight: _____ kg/lbs   Hours Slept: _____ hrs

Sport: _____   Workout: _____

Course: _____   Duration: _____   Distance: _____

Intensity: ☐ Max. Effort   ☐ Hard Effort   ☐ Medium Effort   ☐ Easy Effort

Average HR: _____ bpm   Target HR: _____ bpm

Feeling: ☐ Fantastic   ☐ Good   ☐ Difficult   ☐ Very Difficult

Weather:

Temperature: _____ ° ___   Workout Gear: _____

Notes: _____

_____

_____

Vitals:

Resting HR: _____ bpm   Weight: _____ kg/lbs   Hours Slept: _____ hrs

Sport: _____   Workout: _____

Course: _____   Duration: _____   Distance: _____

Intensity: ☐ Max. Effort   ☐ Hard Effort   ☐ Medium Effort   ☐ Easy Effort

Average HR: _____ bpm   Target HR: _____ bpm

Feeling: ☐ Fantastic   ☐ Good   ☐ Difficult   ☐ Very Difficult

Weather:

Temperature: _____ ° ___   Workout Gear: _____

Notes: _____

_____

_____

Wednesday   Week 11

Vitals:

Resting HR: _____ bpm   Weight: _____ kg/lbs   Hours Slept: _____ hrs

Sport: _____   **Workout:** _____

Course: _____   Duration: _____   Distance: _____

Intensity: ☐ Max. Effort ☐ Hard Effort ☐ Medium Effort ☐ Easy Effort

Average HR: _____ bpm   Target HR: _____ bpm

Feeling: ☐ Fantastic   ☐ Good   ☐ Difficult   ☐ Very Difficult

Weather:

Temperature: _____ ° ___   Workout Gear: _____

Notes: _____
_____
_____

Thursday

Vitals:

Resting HR: _____ bpm   Weight: _____ kg/lbs   Hours Slept: _____ hrs

Sport: _____   **Workout:** _____

Course: _____   Duration: _____   Distance: _____

Intensity: ☐ Max. Effort ☐ Hard Effort ☐ Medium Effort ☐ Easy Effort

Average HR: _____ bpm   Target HR: _____ bpm

Feeling: ☐ Fantastic   ☐ Good   ☐ Difficult   ☐ Very Difficult

Weather:

Temperature: _____ ° ___   Workout Gear: _____

Notes: _____
_____
_____

Friday

Vitals:

Resting HR: _____ bpm   Weight: _____ kg/lbs   Hours Slept: _____ hrs

Sport: _____   **Workout:** _____

Course: _____   Duration: _____   Distance: _____

Intensity: ☐ Max. Effort ☐ Hard Effort ☐ Medium Effort ☐ Easy Effort

Average HR: _____ bpm   Target HR: _____ bpm

Feeling: ☐ Fantastic   ☐ Good   ☐ Difficult   ☐ Very Difficult

Weather:

Temperature: _____ ° ___   Workout Gear: _____

Notes: _____
_____
_____

Vitals:

Resting HR: _____ bpm   Weight: _____ kg/lbs   Hours Slept: _____ hrs

Sport: _____   **Workout:** _____

Course: _____   Duration: _____   Distance: _____

Intensity: ☐ Max. Effort   ☐ Hard Effort   ☐ Medium Effort   ☐ Easy Effort

Average HR: _____ bpm   Target HR: _____ bpm

Feeling: ☐ Fantastic   ☐ Good   ☐ Difficult   ☐ Very Difficult

Weather:

Temperature: _____°_____   Workout Gear: _____

Notes: _____
_____
_____

Week Summary

Total Time: _____ Total Distance: _____

Additional Notes: _____
_____
_____
_____
_____

ANYBODY CAN DO JUST ABOUT
ANYTHING WITH HIMSELF THAT HE
REALLY WANTS TO AND MAKES UP
HIS MIND TO DO. WE ARE CAPABLE
OF GREATER THINGS THAN
WE REALIZE."

— NORMAN VINCENT PEALE

Vitals:

Resting HR: _____ bpm   Weight: _____ kg/lbs   Hours Slept: _____ hrs

Sport: _____   **Workout:** _____

Course: _____   Duration: _____   Distance: _____

Intensity: ☐ Max. Effort   ☐ Hard Effort   ☐ Medium Effort   ☐ Easy Effort

Average HR: _____ bpm   Target HR: _____ bpm

Feeling: ☐ Fantastic   ☐ Good   ☐ Difficult   ☐ Very Difficult

Weather:

Temperature: _____°___   Workout Gear: _____

Notes: _____

_____

_____

Vitals:

Resting HR: _____ bpm   Weight: _____ kg/lbs   Hours Slept: _____ hrs

Sport: _____   **Workout:** _____

Course: _____   Duration: _____   Distance: _____

Intensity: ☐ Max. Effort   ☐ Hard Effort   ☐ Medium Effort   ☐ Easy Effort

Average HR: _____ bpm   Target HR: _____ bpm

Feeling: ☐ Fantastic   ☐ Good   ☐ Difficult   ☐ Very Difficult

Weather:

Temperature: _____°___   Workout Gear: _____

Notes: _____

_____

_____

Vitals:

Resting HR: _____ bpm   Weight: _____ kg/lbs   Hours Slept: _____ hrs

Sport: _____   **Workout:** _____

Course: _____   Duration: _____   Distance: _____

Intensity: ☐ Max. Effort   ☐ Hard Effort   ☐ Medium Effort   ☐ Easy Effort

Average HR: _____ bpm   Target HR: _____ bpm

Feeling: ☐ Fantastic   ☐ Good   ☐ Difficult   ☐ Very Difficult

Weather:

Temperature: _____°___   Workout Gear: _____

Notes: _____

_____

_____

Wednesday   Week 12

Vitals:

Resting HR: _____ bpm   Weight: _____ kg/lbs   Hours Slept: _____ hrs

Sport: _____ **Workout:** _____

Course: _____   Duration: _____   Distance: _____

Intensity: ☐ Max. Effort   ☐ Hard Effort   ☐ Medium Effort   ☐ Easy Effort

Average HR: _____ bpm   Target HR: _____ bpm

Feeling: ☐ Fantastic   ☐ Good   ☐ Difficult   ☐ Very Difficult

Weather:

Temperature: _____ ° ___   Workout Gear: _____

Notes: _____
_____
_____

Thursday

Vitals:

Resting HR: _____ bpm   Weight: _____ kg/lbs   Hours Slept: _____ hrs

Sport: _____ **Workout:** _____

Course: _____   Duration: _____   Distance: _____

Intensity: ☐ Max. Effort   ☐ Hard Effort   ☐ Medium Effort   ☐ Easy Effort

Average HR: _____ bpm   Target HR: _____ bpm

Feeling: ☐ Fantastic   ☐ Good   ☐ Difficult   ☐ Very Difficult

Weather:

Temperature: _____ ° ___   Workout Gear: _____

Notes: _____
_____
_____

Friday

Vitals:

Resting HR: _____ bpm   Weight: _____ kg/lbs   Hours Slept: _____ hrs

Sport: _____ **Workout:** _____

Course: _____   Duration: _____   Distance: _____

Intensity: ☐ Max. Effort   ☐ Hard Effort   ☐ Medium Effort   ☐ Easy Effort

Average HR: _____ bpm   Target HR: _____ bpm

Feeling: ☐ Fantastic   ☐ Good   ☐ Difficult   ☐ Very Difficult

Weather:

Temperature: _____ ° ___   Workout Gear: _____

Notes: _____
_____
_____

Vitals:
Resting HR: _____ bpm   Weight: _____ kg/lbs   Hours Slept: _____ hrs

Sport: _____   Workout: _____

Course: _____   Duration: _____   Distance: _____

Intensity: ☐ Max. Effort ☐ Hard Effort ☐ Medium Effort ☐ Easy Effort

Average HR: _____ bpm   Target HR: _____ bpm

Feeling: ☐ Fantastic ☐ Good ☐ Difficult ☐ Very Difficult

Weather:
Temperature: _____ ° ___   Workout Gear: _____

Notes: _____
_____
_____

Week Summary

Distance / Time

Sunday   Monday   Tuesday   Wednesday   Thursday   Friday   Saturday

Day

Total Time: _____ Total Distance: _____

Additional Notes: _____
_____
_____
_____
_____
_____

Vitals:
Resting HR: _____ bpm   Weight: _____ kg/lbs   Hours Slept: _____ hrs

Sport: _____ **Workout:** _____

Course: _____   Duration: _____   Distance: _____

Intensity: ☐ Max. Effort   ☐ Hard Effort   ☐ Medium Effort   ☐ Easy Effort

Average HR: _____ bpm   Target HR: _____ bpm

Feeling: ☐ Fantastic   ☐ Good   ☐ Difficult   ☐ Very Difficult

Weather:
Temperature: _____ ° ___   Workout Gear: _____

Notes: _____
_____
_____

Monday

Vitals:
Resting HR: _____ bpm   Weight: _____ kg/lbs   Hours Slept: _____ hrs

Sport: _____ **Workout:** _____

Course: _____   Duration: _____   Distance: _____

Intensity: ☐ Max. Effort   ☐ Hard Effort   ☐ Medium Effort   ☐ Easy Effort

Average HR: _____ bpm   Target HR: _____ bpm

Feeling: ☐ Fantastic   ☐ Good   ☐ Difficult   ☐ Very Difficult

Weather:
Temperature: _____ ° ___   Workout Gear: _____

Notes: _____
_____
_____

Tuesday

Vitals:
Resting HR: _____ bpm   Weight: _____ kg/lbs   Hours Slept: _____ hrs

Sport: _____ **Workout:** _____

Course: _____   Duration: _____   Distance: _____

Intensity: ☐ Max. Effort   ☐ Hard Effort   ☐ Medium Effort   ☐ Easy Effort

Average HR: _____ bpm   Target HR: _____ bpm

Feeling: ☐ Fantastic   ☐ Good   ☐ Difficult   ☐ Very Difficult

Weather:
Temperature: _____ ° ___   Workout Gear: _____

Notes: _____
_____
_____

Vitals:

Resting HR: _____ bpm   Weight: _____ kg/lbs   Hours Slept: _____ hrs

Sport: _____   **Workout:** _____

Course: _____   Duration: _____   Distance: _____

Intensity: ☐ Max. Effort   ☐ Hard Effort   ☐ Medium Effort   ☐ Easy Effort

Average HR: _____ bpm   Target HR: _____ bpm

Feeling: ☐ Fantastic   ☐ Good   ☐ Difficult   ☐ Very Difficult

Weather:

Temperature: _____ ° ___   Workout Gear: _____

Notes: _____
_____
_____

Thursday

Vitals:

Resting HR: _____ bpm   Weight: _____ kg/lbs   Hours Slept: _____ hrs

Sport: _____   **Workout:** _____

Course: _____   Duration: _____   Distance: _____

Intensity: ☐ Max. Effort   ☐ Hard Effort   ☐ Medium Effort   ☐ Easy Effort

Average HR: _____ bpm   Target HR: _____ bpm

Feeling: ☐ Fantastic   ☐ Good   ☐ Difficult   ☐ Very Difficult

Weather:

Temperature: _____ ° ___   Workout Gear: _____

Notes: _____
_____
_____

Friday

Vitals:

Resting HR: _____ bpm   Weight: _____ kg/lbs   Hours Slept: _____ hrs

Sport: _____   **Workout:** _____

Course: _____   Duration: _____   Distance: _____

Intensity: ☐ Max. Effort   ☐ Hard Effort   ☐ Medium Effort   ☐ Easy Effort

Average HR: _____ bpm   Target HR: _____ bpm

Feeling: ☐ Fantastic   ☐ Good   ☐ Difficult   ☐ Very Difficult

Weather:

Temperature: _____ ° ___   Workout Gear: _____

Notes: _____
_____
_____

Vitals:

Resting HR: _____ bpm   Weight: _____ kg/lbs   Hours Slept: _____ hrs

Sport: _____   Workout: _____

Course: _____   Duration: _____   Distance: _____

Intensity: ☐ Max. Effort   ☐ Hard Effort   ☐ Medium Effort   ☐ Easy Effort

Average HR: _____ bpm   Target HR: _____ bpm

Feeling: ☐ Fantastic   ☐ Good   ☐ Difficult   ☐ Very Difficult

Weather:

Temperature: _____ ° ___   Workout Gear: _____

Notes: _____

_____

_____

Week Summary

	Sunday	Monday	Tuesday	Wednesday	Thursday	Friday	Saturday

Distance / Time (vertical axis)

Day

Total Time: _____ Total Distance: _____

Additional Notes: _____

_____

_____

_____

_____

_____

"A healthy body is a guest-chamber for the soul, a sick body is a prison."

— Francis Bacon

Week 14   Date: ☐ ☐ ☐   Sunday

Vitals:

Resting HR: _____ bpm   Weight: _____ kg/lbs   Hours Slept: _____ hrs

Sport: _____   **Workout:** _____

Course: _____   Duration: _____   Distance: _____

Intensity: ☐ Max. Effort ☐ Hard Effort ☐ Medium Effort ☐ Easy Effort

Average HR: _____ bpm   Target HR: _____ bpm

Feeling: ☐ Fantastic ☐ Good ☐ Difficult ☐ Very Difficult

Weather:

Temperature: _____ ° ___   Workout Gear: _____

Notes: _____

_____

_____

Monday

Vitals:

Resting HR: _____ bpm   Weight: _____ kg/lbs   Hours Slept: _____ hrs

Sport: _____   **Workout:** _____

Course: _____   Duration: _____   Distance: _____

Intensity: ☐ Max. Effort ☐ Hard Effort ☐ Medium Effort ☐ Easy Effort

Average HR: _____ bpm   Target HR: _____ bpm

Feeling: ☐ Fantastic ☐ Good ☐ Difficult ☐ Very Difficult

Weather:

Temperature: _____ ° ___   Workout Gear: _____

Notes: _____

_____

_____

Tuesday

Vitals:

Resting HR: _____ bpm   Weight: _____ kg/lbs   Hours Slept: _____ hrs

Sport: _____   **Workout:** _____

Course: _____   Duration: _____   Distance: _____

Intensity: ☐ Max. Effort ☐ Hard Effort ☐ Medium Effort ☐ Easy Effort

Average HR: _____ bpm   Target HR: _____ bpm

Feeling: ☐ Fantastic ☐ Good ☐ Difficult ☐ Very Difficult

Weather:

Temperature: _____ ° ___   Workout Gear: _____

Notes: _____

_____

_____

Wednesday

Vitals:

Resting HR: _____ bpm   Weight: _____ kg/lbs   Hours Slept: _____ hrs

Sport: _____   **Workout:** _____

Course: _____   Duration: _____   Distance: _____

Intensity: ☐ Max. Effort   ☐ Hard Effort   ☐ Medium Effort   ☐ Easy Effort

Average HR: _____ bpm   Target HR: _____ bpm

Feeling: ☐ Fantastic   ☐ Good   ☐ Difficult   ☐ Very Difficult

Weather:

Temperature: _____ ° ___   Workout Gear: _____

Notes: _____

_____

_____

Thursday

Vitals:

Resting HR: _____ bpm   Weight: _____ kg/lbs   Hours Slept: _____ hrs

Sport: _____   **Workout:** _____

Course: _____   Duration: _____   Distance: _____

Intensity: ☐ Max. Effort   ☐ Hard Effort   ☐ Medium Effort   ☐ Easy Effort

Average HR: _____ bpm   Target HR: _____ bpm

Feeling: ☐ Fantastic   ☐ Good   ☐ Difficult   ☐ Very Difficult

Weather:

Temperature: _____ ° ___   Workout Gear: _____

Notes: _____

_____

_____

Friday

Vitals:

Resting HR: _____ bpm   Weight: _____ kg/lbs   Hours Slept: _____ hrs

Sport: _____   **Workout:** _____

Course: _____   Duration: _____   Distance: _____

Intensity: ☐ Max. Effort   ☐ Hard Effort   ☐ Medium Effort   ☐ Easy Effort

Average HR: _____ bpm   Target HR: _____ bpm

Feeling: ☐ Fantastic   ☐ Good   ☐ Difficult   ☐ Very Difficult

Weather:

Temperature: _____ ° ___   Workout Gear: _____

Notes: _____

_____

_____

Vitals:

Resting HR: _____ bpm   Weight: _____ kg/lbs   Hours Slept: _____ hrs

Sport: _____   **Workout:** _____

Course: _____   Duration: _____   Distance: _____

Intensity: ☐ Max. Effort ☐ Hard Effort ☐ Medium Effort ☐ Easy Effort

Average HR: _____ bpm   Target HR: _____ bpm

Feeling: ☐ Fantastic ☐ Good ☐ Difficult ☐ Very Difficult

Weather:

Temperature: _____ ° ___   Workout Gear: _____

Notes: _____
_____
_____

Week Summary

Total Time: _____ Total Distance: _____

Additional Notes: _____
_____
_____
_____
_____

" there are clubs you can't belong to , neighborhoods you can't LIVE in , schools you CAN'T GET into , but THE Roads are ALWAYS OPEN ."

= NIKE

Vitals:

Resting HR: _____ bpm   Weight: _____ kg/lbs   Hours Slept: _____ hrs

Sport: _____   **Workout:** _____

Course: _____   Duration: _____   Distance: _____

Intensity: ☐ Max. Effort   ☐ Hard Effort   ☐ Medium Effort   ☐ Easy Effort

Average HR: _____ bpm   Target HR: _____ bpm

Feeling: ☐ Fantastic   ☐ Good   ☐ Difficult   ☐ Very Difficult

Weather:

Temperature: _____ ° ___   Workout Gear: _____

Notes: _____
_____
_____

Monday

Vitals:

Resting HR: _____ bpm   Weight: _____ kg/lbs   Hours Slept: _____ hrs

Sport: _____   **Workout:** _____

Course: _____   Duration: _____   Distance: _____

Intensity: ☐ Max. Effort   ☐ Hard Effort   ☐ Medium Effort   ☐ Easy Effort

Average HR: _____ bpm   Target HR: _____ bpm

Feeling: ☐ Fantastic   ☐ Good   ☐ Difficult   ☐ Very Difficult

Weather:

Temperature: _____ ° ___   Workout Gear: _____

Notes: _____
_____
_____

Tuesday

Vitals:

Resting HR: _____ bpm   Weight: _____ kg/lbs   Hours Slept: _____ hrs

Sport: _____   **Workout:** _____

Course: _____   Duration: _____   Distance: _____

Intensity: ☐ Max. Effort   ☐ Hard Effort   ☐ Medium Effort   ☐ Easy Effort

Average HR: _____ bpm   Target HR: _____ bpm

Feeling: ☐ Fantastic   ☐ Good   ☐ Difficult   ☐ Very Difficult

Weather:

Temperature: _____ ° ___   Workout Gear: _____

Notes: _____
_____
_____

Vitals:

Resting HR: _____ bpm   Weight: _____ kg/lbs   Hours Slept: _____ hrs

Sport: _____   **Workout:** _____

Course: _____   Duration: _____   Distance: _____

Intensity: ☐ Max. Effort   ☐ Hard Effort   ☐ Medium Effort   ☐ Easy Effort

Average HR: _____ bpm   Target HR: _____ bpm

Feeling: ☐ Fantastic   ☐ Good   ☐ Difficult   ☐ Very Difficult

Weather:

Temperature: _____ ° ___   Workout Gear: _____

Notes: _____

_____

_____

Thursday

Vitals:

Resting HR: _____ bpm   Weight: _____ kg/lbs   Hours Slept: _____ hrs

Sport: _____   **Workout:** _____

Course: _____   Duration: _____   Distance: _____

Intensity: ☐ Max. Effort   ☐ Hard Effort   ☐ Medium Effort   ☐ Easy Effort

Average HR: _____ bpm   Target HR: _____ bpm

Feeling: ☐ Fantastic   ☐ Good   ☐ Difficult   ☐ Very Difficult

Weather:

Temperature: _____ ° ___   Workout Gear: _____

Notes: _____

_____

_____

Friday

Vitals:

Resting HR: _____ bpm   Weight: _____ kg/lbs   Hours Slept: _____ hrs

Sport: _____   **Workout:** _____

Course: _____   Duration: _____   Distance: _____

Intensity: ☐ Max. Effort   ☐ Hard Effort   ☐ Medium Effort   ☐ Easy Effort

Average HR: _____ bpm   Target HR: _____ bpm

Feeling: ☐ Fantastic   ☐ Good   ☐ Difficult   ☐ Very Difficult

Weather:

Temperature: _____ ° ___   Workout Gear: _____

Notes: _____

_____

_____

Vitals:

Resting HR: _____ bpm   Weight: _____ kg/lbs   Hours Slept: _____ hrs

Sport: _____   Workout: _____

Course: _____   Duration: _____   Distance: _____

Intensity: ▢ Max. Effort   ▢ Hard Effort   ▢ Medium Effort   ▢ Easy Effort

Average HR: _____ bpm   Target HR: _____ bpm

Feeling: ▢ Fantastic   ▢ Good   ▢ Difficult   ▢ Very Difficult

Weather:

Temperature: _____ ° ___   Workout Gear: _____

Notes: _____

_____

_____

Week Summary

Distance / Time (y-axis)

Sunday   Monday   Tuesday   Wednesday   Thursday   Friday   Saturday

Day

Total Time: _____ Total Distance: _____

Additional Notes: _____

_____

_____

_____

_____

_____

"RUNNERS JUST DO IT—THEY RUN FOR THE FINISH LINE EVEN IF SOMEONE ELSE HAS REACHED IT FIRST." — ANONYMOUS

Vitals:

Resting HR: _____ bpm   Weight: _____ kg/lbs   Hours Slept: _____ hrs

Sport: _____   **Workout:** _____

Course: _____   Duration: _____   Distance: _____

Intensity: ☐ Max. Effort   ☐ Hard Effort   ☐ Medium Effort   ☐ Easy Effort

Average HR: _____ bpm   Target HR: _____ bpm

Feeling: ☐ Fantastic   ☐ Good   ☐ Difficult   ☐ Very Difficult

Weather:

Temperature: _____ ° ___   Workout Gear: _____

Notes: _____

_____

_____

Monday

Vitals:

Resting HR: _____ bpm   Weight: _____ kg/lbs   Hours Slept: _____ hrs

Sport: _____   **Workout:** _____

Course: _____   Duration: _____   Distance: _____

Intensity: ☐ Max. Effort   ☐ Hard Effort   ☐ Medium Effort   ☐ Easy Effort

Average HR: _____ bpm   Target HR: _____ bpm

Feeling: ☐ Fantastic   ☐ Good   ☐ Difficult   ☐ Very Difficult

Weather:

Temperature: _____ ° ___   Workout Gear: _____

Notes: _____

_____

_____

Tuesday

Vitals:

Resting HR: _____ bpm   Weight: _____ kg/lbs   Hours Slept: _____ hrs

Sport: _____   **Workout:** _____

Course: _____   Duration: _____   Distance: _____

Intensity: ☐ Max. Effort   ☐ Hard Effort   ☐ Medium Effort   ☐ Easy Effort

Average HR: _____ bpm   Target HR: _____ bpm

Feeling: ☐ Fantastic   ☐ Good   ☐ Difficult   ☐ Very Difficult

Weather:

Temperature: _____ ° ___   Workout Gear: _____

Notes: _____

_____

_____

Vitals:

Resting HR: _____ bpm   Weight: _____ kg/lbs   Hours Slept: _____ hrs

Sport: _____   **Workout:** _____

Course: _____   Duration: _____   Distance: _____

Intensity: ☐ Max. Effort   ☐ Hard Effort   ☐ Medium Effort   ☐ Easy Effort

Average HR: _____ bpm   Target HR: _____ bpm

Feeling: ☐ Fantastic   ☐ Good   ☐ Difficult   ☐ Very Difficult

Weather:

Temperature: _____ ° ___   Workout Gear: _____

Notes: _____

_____

_____

Thursday

Vitals:

Resting HR: _____ bpm   Weight: _____ kg/lbs   Hours Slept: _____ hrs

Sport: _____   **Workout:** _____

Course: _____   Duration: _____   Distance: _____

Intensity: ☐ Max. Effort   ☐ Hard Effort   ☐ Medium Effort   ☐ Easy Effort

Average HR: _____ bpm   Target HR: _____ bpm

Feeling: ☐ Fantastic   ☐ Good   ☐ Difficult   ☐ Very Difficult

Weather:

Temperature: _____ ° ___   Workout Gear: _____

Notes: _____

_____

_____

Friday

Vitals:

Resting HR: _____ bpm   Weight: _____ kg/lbs   Hours Slept: _____ hrs

Sport: _____   **Workout:** _____

Course: _____   Duration: _____   Distance: _____

Intensity: ☐ Max. Effort   ☐ Hard Effort   ☐ Medium Effort   ☐ Easy Effort

Average HR: _____ bpm   Target HR: _____ bpm

Feeling: ☐ Fantastic   ☐ Good   ☐ Difficult   ☐ Very Difficult

Weather:

Temperature: _____ ° ___   Workout Gear: _____

Notes: _____

_____

_____

Vitals:

Resting HR: _____ bpm   Weight: _____ kg/lbs   Hours Slept: _____ hrs

Sport: _____   Workout: _____

Course: _____   Duration: _____   Distance: _____

Intensity: ☐ Max. Effort   ☐ Hard Effort   ☐ Medium Effort   ☐ Easy Effort

Average HR: _____ bpm   Target HR: _____ bpm

Feeling: ☐ Fantastic   ☐ Good   ☐ Difficult   ☐ Very Difficult

Weather:

Temperature: _____ ° _____   Workout Gear: _____

Notes: _____

_____

_____

Week Summary

Total Time: _____ Total Distance: _____

Additional Notes: _____

_____

_____

_____

_____

_____

"Running is not about competing. It is about improving one's health."
— John Stanton

Vitals:

Resting HR: _____ bpm   Weight: _____ kg/lbs   Hours Slept: _____ hrs

Sport: _____   **Workout:** _____

Course: _____   Duration: _____   Distance: _____

Intensity: ☐ Max. Effort   ☐ Hard Effort   ☐ Medium Effort   ☐ Easy Effort

Average HR: _____ bpm   Target HR: _____ bpm

Feeling: ☐ Fantastic   ☐ Good   ☐ Difficult   ☐ Very Difficult

Weather:

Temperature: _____°___   Workout Gear: _____

Notes: _____

_____

_____

Monday

Vitals:

Resting HR: _____ bpm   Weight: _____ kg/lbs   Hours Slept: _____ hrs

Sport: _____   **Workout:** _____

Course: _____   Duration: _____   Distance: _____

Intensity: ☐ Max. Effort   ☐ Hard Effort   ☐ Medium Effort   ☐ Easy Effort

Average HR: _____ bpm   Target HR: _____ bpm

Feeling: ☐ Fantastic   ☐ Good   ☐ Difficult   ☐ Very Difficult

Weather:

Temperature: _____°___   Workout Gear: _____

Notes: _____

_____

_____

Tuesday

Vitals:

Resting HR: _____ bpm   Weight: _____ kg/lbs   Hours Slept: _____ hrs

Sport: _____   **Workout:** _____

Course: _____   Duration: _____   Distance: _____

Intensity: ☐ Max. Effort   ☐ Hard Effort   ☐ Medium Effort   ☐ Easy Effort

Average HR: _____ bpm   Target HR: _____ bpm

Feeling: ☐ Fantastic   ☐ Good   ☐ Difficult   ☐ Very Difficult

Weather:

Temperature: _____°___   Workout Gear: _____

Notes: _____

_____

_____

Vitals:

Resting HR: _____ bpm   Weight: _____ kg/lbs   Hours Slept: _____ hrs

Sport: _____   **Workout:** _____

Course: _____   Duration: _____   Distance: _____

Intensity: ☐ Max. Effort   ☐ Hard Effort   ☐ Medium Effort   ☐ Easy Effort

Average HR: _____ bpm   Target HR: _____ bpm

Feeling: ☐ Fantastic   ☐ Good   ☐ Difficult   ☐ Very Difficult

Weather:

Temperature: _____ ° ___   Workout Gear: _____

Notes: _____

_____

_____

Thursday

Vitals:

Resting HR: _____ bpm   Weight: _____ kg/lbs   Hours Slept: _____ hrs

Sport: _____   **Workout:** _____

Course: _____   Duration: _____   Distance: _____

Intensity: ☐ Max. Effort   ☐ Hard Effort   ☐ Medium Effort   ☐ Easy Effort

Average HR: _____ bpm   Target HR: _____ bpm

Feeling: ☐ Fantastic   ☐ Good   ☐ Difficult   ☐ Very Difficult

Weather:

Temperature: _____ ° ___   Workout Gear: _____

Notes: _____

_____

_____

Friday

Vitals:

Resting HR: _____ bpm   Weight: _____ kg/lbs   Hours Slept: _____ hrs

Sport: _____   **Workout:** _____

Course: _____   Duration: _____   Distance: _____

Intensity: ☐ Max. Effort   ☐ Hard Effort   ☐ Medium Effort   ☐ Easy Effort

Average HR: _____ bpm   Target HR: _____ bpm

Feeling: ☐ Fantastic   ☐ Good   ☐ Difficult   ☐ Very Difficult

Weather:

Temperature: _____ ° ___   Workout Gear: _____

Notes: _____

_____

_____

Vitals:

Resting HR: _____ bpm   Weight: _____ kg/lbs   Hours Slept: _____ hrs

Sport: _____ **Workout:** _____

Course: _____   Duration: _____   Distance: _____

Intensity: ☐ Max. Effort   ☐ Hard Effort   ☐ Medium Effort   ☐ Easy Effort

Average HR: _____ bpm   Target HR: _____ bpm

Feeling: ☐ Fantastic   ☐ Good   ☐ Difficult   ☐ Very Difficult

Weather:

Temperature: _____ ° ___   Workout Gear: _____

Notes: _____

_____

_____

Week Summary

Distance / Time

Sunday   Monday   Tuesday   Wednesday   Thursday   Friday   Saturday

Day

Total Time: _____ Total Distance: _____

Additional Notes: _____

_____

_____

_____

_____

"Quitters take bad breaks and use them as reasons to give up." — Nancy Lopez

Vitals:

Resting HR: _____ bpm   Weight: _____ kg/lbs   Hours Slept: _____ hrs

Sport: _____   **Workout:** _____

Course: _____   Duration: _____   Distance: _____

Intensity: ☐ Max. Effort   ☐ Hard Effort   ☐ Medium Effort   ☐ Easy Effort

Average HR: _____ bpm   Target HR: _____ bpm

Feeling: ☐ Fantastic   ☐ Good   ☐ Difficult   ☐ Very Difficult

Weather:

Temperature: _____ ° ___   Workout Gear: _____

Notes: _____

_____

_____

Vitals:

Resting HR: _____ bpm   Weight: _____ kg/lbs   Hours Slept: _____ hrs

Sport: _____   **Workout:** _____

Course: _____   Duration: _____   Distance: _____

Intensity: ☐ Max. Effort   ☐ Hard Effort   ☐ Medium Effort   ☐ Easy Effort

Average HR: _____ bpm   Target HR: _____ bpm

Feeling: ☐ Fantastic   ☐ Good   ☐ Difficult   ☐ Very Difficult

Weather:

Temperature: _____ ° ___   Workout Gear: _____

Notes: _____

_____

_____

Vitals:

Resting HR: _____ bpm   Weight: _____ kg/lbs   Hours Slept: _____ hrs

Sport: _____   **Workout:** _____

Course: _____   Duration: _____   Distance: _____

Intensity: ☐ Max. Effort   ☐ Hard Effort   ☐ Medium Effort   ☐ Easy Effort

Average HR: _____ bpm   Target HR: _____ bpm

Feeling: ☐ Fantastic   ☐ Good   ☐ Difficult   ☐ Very Difficult

Weather:

Temperature: _____ ° ___   Workout Gear: _____

Notes: _____

_____

_____

Wednesday   Week 18

Vitals:

Resting HR: _____ bpm   Weight: _____ kg/lbs   Hours Slept: _____ hrs

Sport: _____   **Workout:** _____

Course: _____   Duration: _____   Distance: _____

Intensity: ☐ Max. Effort   ☐ Hard Effort   ☐ Medium Effort   ☐ Easy Effort

Average HR: _____ bpm   Target HR: _____ bpm

Feeling: ☐ Fantastic   ☐ Good   ☐ Difficult   ☐ Very Difficult

Weather:

Temperature: _____°____   Workout Gear: _____

Notes: _____
_____
_____

Thursday

Vitals:

Resting HR: _____ bpm   Weight: _____ kg/lbs   Hours Slept: _____ hrs

Sport: _____   **Workout:** _____

Course: _____   Duration: _____   Distance: _____

Intensity: ☐ Max. Effort   ☐ Hard Effort   ☐ Medium Effort   ☐ Easy Effort

Average HR: _____ bpm   Target HR: _____ bpm

Feeling: ☐ Fantastic   ☐ Good   ☐ Difficult   ☐ Very Difficult

Weather:

Temperature: _____°____   Workout Gear: _____

Notes: _____
_____
_____

Friday

Vitals:

Resting HR: _____ bpm   Weight: _____ kg/lbs   Hours Slept: _____ hrs

Sport: _____   **Workout:** _____

Course: _____   Duration: _____   Distance: _____

Intensity: ☐ Max. Effort   ☐ Hard Effort   ☐ Medium Effort   ☐ Easy Effort

Average HR: _____ bpm   Target HR: _____ bpm

Feeling: ☐ Fantastic   ☐ Good   ☐ Difficult   ☐ Very Difficult

Weather:

Temperature: _____°____   Workout Gear: _____

Notes: _____
_____
_____

Week 18 Date: ▮▮ ▮▮ ▮▮ Saturday

Vitals:

Resting HR: _____ bpm   Weight: _____ kg/lbs   Hours Slept: _____ hrs

Sport: _____ **Workout:** _____

Course: _____   Duration: _____   Distance: _____

Intensity: ☐ Max. Effort   ☐ Hard Effort   ☐ Medium Effort   ☐ Easy Effort

Average HR: _____ bpm   Target HR: _____ bpm

Feeling: ☐ Fantastic   ☐ Good   ☐ Difficult   ☐ Very Difficult

Weather:

Temperature: _____ ° ___   Workout Gear: _____

Notes: _____

_____

_____

Week Summary

Total Time: _____ Total Distance: _____

Additional Notes: _____

_____

_____

_____

_____

_____

"The most important thing in the Olympic Games is not to win but to take part, just as the most important thing in life is not the triumph but the struggle."

— Baron de Coubertin, founder of the modern Olympic Games, 1890

Vitals:

Resting HR: _____ bpm   Weight: _____ kg/lbs   Hours Slept: _____ hrs

Sport: _____   **Workout:** _____

Course: _____   Duration: _____   Distance: _____

Intensity: ☐ Max. Effort   ☐ Hard Effort   ☐ Medium Effort   ☐ Easy Effort

Average HR: _____ bpm   Target HR: _____ bpm

Feeling: ☐ Fantastic   ☐ Good   ☐ Difficult   ☐ Very Difficult

Weather:

Temperature: _____ ° ___   Workout Gear: _____

Notes: _____

_____

_____

Monday

Vitals:

Resting HR: _____ bpm   Weight: _____ kg/lbs   Hours Slept: _____ hrs

Sport: _____   **Workout:** _____

Course: _____   Duration: _____   Distance: _____

Intensity: ☐ Max. Effort   ☐ Hard Effort   ☐ Medium Effort   ☐ Easy Effort

Average HR: _____ bpm   Target HR: _____ bpm

Feeling: ☐ Fantastic   ☐ Good   ☐ Difficult   ☐ Very Difficult

Weather:

Temperature: _____ ° ___   Workout Gear: _____

Notes: _____

_____

_____

Tuesday

Vitals:

Resting HR: _____ bpm   Weight: _____ kg/lbs   Hours Slept: _____ hrs

Sport: _____   **Workout:** _____

Course: _____   Duration: _____   Distance: _____

Intensity: ☐ Max. Effort   ☐ Hard Effort   ☐ Medium Effort   ☐ Easy Effort

Average HR: _____ bpm   Target HR: _____ bpm

Feeling: ☐ Fantastic   ☐ Good   ☐ Difficult   ☐ Very Difficult

Weather:

Temperature: _____ ° ___   Workout Gear: _____

Notes: _____

_____

_____

Wednesday   Week 19

Vitals:

Resting HR: _____ bpm   Weight: _____ kg/lbs   Hours Slept: _____ hrs

Sport: _____   **Workout:** _____

Course: _____   Duration: _____   Distance: _____

Intensity: ☐ Max. Effort   ☐ Hard Effort   ☐ Medium Effort   ☐ Easy Effort

Average HR: _____ bpm   Target HR: _____ bpm

Feeling: ☐ Fantastic   ☐ Good   ☐ Difficult   ☐ Very Difficult

Weather:

Temperature: _____ ° ___   Workout Gear: _____

Notes: _____

_____

_____

Thursday

Vitals:

Resting HR: _____ bpm   Weight: _____ kg/lbs   Hours Slept: _____ hrs

Sport: _____   **Workout:** _____

Course: _____   Duration: _____   Distance: _____

Intensity: ☐ Max. Effort   ☐ Hard Effort   ☐ Medium Effort   ☐ Easy Effort

Average HR: _____ bpm   Target HR: _____ bpm

Feeling: ☐ Fantastic   ☐ Good   ☐ Difficult   ☐ Very Difficult

Weather:

Temperature: _____ ° ___   Workout Gear: _____

Notes: _____

_____

_____

Friday

Vitals:

Resting HR: _____ bpm   Weight: _____ kg/lbs   Hours Slept: _____ hrs

Sport: _____   **Workout:** _____

Course: _____   Duration: _____   Distance: _____

Intensity: ☐ Max. Effort   ☐ Hard Effort   ☐ Medium Effort   ☐ Easy Effort

Average HR: _____ bpm   Target HR: _____ bpm

Feeling: ☐ Fantastic   ☐ Good   ☐ Difficult   ☐ Very Difficult

Weather:

Temperature: _____ ° ___   Workout Gear: _____

Notes: _____

_____

_____

Vitals:

Resting HR: _____ bpm   Weight: _____ kg/lbs   Hours Slept: _____ hrs

Sport: _____   **Workout:** _____

Course: _____   Duration: _____   Distance: _____

Intensity: ▢ Max. Effort   ▢ Hard Effort   ▢ Medium Effort   ▢ Easy Effort

Average HR: _____ bpm   Target HR: _____ bpm

Feeling: ▢ Fantastic   ▢ Good   ▢ Difficult   ▢ Very Difficult

Weather:

Temperature: _____ ° ___   Workout Gear: _____

Notes: _____

_____

_____

Week Summary

Distance / Time (y-axis)

Sunday   Monday   Tuesday   Wednesday   Thursday   Friday   Saturday

Day

Total Time: _____ Total Distance: _____

Additional Notes: _____

_____

_____

_____

_____

_____

44 LIFESTYLE

"Everyone who has run knows that its most important value is in removing tension and allowing a release from whatever other cares the day may bring." — Jimmy Carter

Vitals:

Resting HR: _____ bpm   Weight: _____ kg/lbs   Hours Slept: _____ hrs

Sport: _____   **Workout:** _____

Course: _____   Duration: _____   Distance: _____

Intensity: ☐ Max. Effort ☐ Hard Effort ☐ Medium Effort ☐ Easy Effort

Average HR: _____ bpm   Target HR: _____ bpm

Feeling: ☐ Fantastic ☐ Good ☐ Difficult ☐ Very Difficult

Weather:

Temperature: _____ ° ___   Workout Gear: _____

Notes: _____

_____

_____

Monday

Vitals:

Resting HR: _____ bpm   Weight: _____ kg/lbs   Hours Slept: _____ hrs

Sport: _____   **Workout:** _____

Course: _____   Duration: _____   Distance: _____

Intensity: ☐ Max. Effort ☐ Hard Effort ☐ Medium Effort ☐ Easy Effort

Average HR: _____ bpm   Target HR: _____ bpm

Feeling: ☐ Fantastic ☐ Good ☐ Difficult ☐ Very Difficult

Weather:

Temperature: _____ ° ___   Workout Gear: _____

Notes: _____

_____

_____

Tuesday

Vitals:

Resting HR: _____ bpm   Weight: _____ kg/lbs   Hours Slept: _____ hrs

Sport: _____   **Workout:** _____

Course: _____   Duration: _____   Distance: _____

Intensity: ☐ Max. Effort ☐ Hard Effort ☐ Medium Effort ☐ Easy Effort

Average HR: _____ bpm   Target HR: _____ bpm

Feeling: ☐ Fantastic ☐ Good ☐ Difficult ☐ Very Difficult

Weather:

Temperature: _____ ° ___   Workout Gear: _____

Notes: _____

_____

_____

Vitals:

Resting HR: _____ bpm   Weight: _____ kg/lbs   Hours Slept: _____ hrs

Sport: _____ **Workout:** _____

Course: _____   Duration: _____   Distance: _____

Intensity: ☐ Max. Effort ☐ Hard Effort ☐ Medium Effort ☐ Easy Effort

Average HR: _____ bpm   Target HR: _____ bpm

Feeling: ☐ Fantastic   ☐ Good   ☐ Difficult   ☐ Very Difficult

Weather:

Temperature: _____ ° ___   Workout Gear: _____

Notes: _____
_____
_____

Thursday

Vitals:

Resting HR: _____ bpm   Weight: _____ kg/lbs   Hours Slept: _____ hrs

Sport: _____ **Workout:** _____

Course: _____   Duration: _____   Distance: _____

Intensity: ☐ Max. Effort ☐ Hard Effort ☐ Medium Effort ☐ Easy Effort

Average HR: _____ bpm   Target HR: _____ bpm

Feeling: ☐ Fantastic   ☐ Good   ☐ Difficult   ☐ Very Difficult

Weather:

Temperature: _____ ° ___   Workout Gear: _____

Notes: _____
_____
_____

Friday

Vitals:

Resting HR: _____ bpm   Weight: _____ kg/lbs   Hours Slept: _____ hrs

Sport: _____ **Workout:** _____

Course: _____   Duration: _____   Distance: _____

Intensity: ☐ Max. Effort ☐ Hard Effort ☐ Medium Effort ☐ Easy Effort

Average HR: _____ bpm   Target HR: _____ bpm

Feeling: ☐ Fantastic   ☐ Good   ☐ Difficult   ☐ Very Difficult

Weather:

Temperature: _____ ° ___   Workout Gear: _____

Notes: _____
_____
_____

Week 20   Date: ▮ ▮ ▮   Saturday

Vitals:

Resting HR: _____ bpm   Weight: _____ kg/lbs   Hours Slept: _____ hrs

Sport: _____   **Workout:** _____

Course: _____   Duration: _____   Distance: _____

Intensity: ☐ Max. Effort ☐ Hard Effort ☐ Medium Effort ☐ Easy Effort

Average HR: _____ bpm   Target HR: _____ bpm

Feeling: ☐ Fantastic ☐ Good ☐ Difficult ☐ Very Difficult

Weather:

Temperature: _____ ° ___   Workout Gear: _____

Notes: _____

_____

_____

Week Summary

Total Time: _____ Total Distance: _____

Additional Notes: _____

_____

_____

_____

_____

"Luck has nothing
to do with it."
— Anonymous

Vitals:

Resting HR: _____ bpm　　Weight: _____ kg/lbs　Hours Slept: _____ hrs

Sport: _____　**Workout:** _____

Course: _____　　Duration: _____　　Distance: _____

Intensity:　☐ Max. Effort　☐ Hard Effort　☐ Medium Effort　☐ Easy Effort

Average HR: _____ bpm　　Target HR: _____ bpm

Feeling:　☐ Fantastic　☐ Good　☐ Difficult　☐ Very Difficult

Weather:

Temperature: _____ ° ___　　Workout Gear: _____

Notes: _____

_____

_____

Monday

Vitals:

Resting HR: _____ bpm　　Weight: _____ kg/lbs　Hours Slept: _____ hrs

Sport: _____　**Workout:** _____

Course: _____　　Duration: _____　　Distance: _____

Intensity:　☐ Max. Effort　☐ Hard Effort　☐ Medium Effort　☐ Easy Effort

Average HR: _____ bpm　　Target HR: _____ bpm

Feeling:　☐ Fantastic　☐ Good　☐ Difficult　☐ Very Difficult

Weather:

Temperature: _____ ° ___　　Workout Gear: _____

Notes: _____

_____

_____

Tuesday

Vitals:

Resting HR: _____ bpm　　Weight: _____ kg/lbs　Hours Slept: _____ hrs

Sport: _____　**Workout:** _____

Course: _____　　Duration: _____　　Distance: _____

Intensity:　☐ Max. Effort　☐ Hard Effort　☐ Medium Effort　☐ Easy Effort

Average HR: _____ bpm　　Target HR: _____ bpm

Feeling:　☐ Fantastic　☐ Good　☐ Difficult　☐ Very Difficult

Weather:

Temperature: _____ ° ___　　Workout Gear: _____

Notes: _____

_____

_____

Vitals:

Resting HR: _____ bpm   Weight: _____ kg/lbs   Hours Slept: _____ hrs

Sport: _____   **Workout:** _____

Course: _____   Duration: _____   Distance: _____

Intensity: ☐ Max. Effort   ☐ Hard Effort   ☐ Medium Effort   ☐ Easy Effort

Average HR: _____ bpm   Target HR: _____ bpm

Feeling: ☐ Fantastic   ☐ Good   ☐ Difficult   ☐ Very Difficult

Weather:

Temperature: _____°___   Workout Gear: _____

Notes: _____
_____
_____

Thursday

Vitals:

Resting HR: _____ bpm   Weight: _____ kg/lbs   Hours Slept: _____ hrs

Sport: _____   **Workout:** _____

Course: _____   Duration: _____   Distance: _____

Intensity: ☐ Max. Effort   ☐ Hard Effort   ☐ Medium Effort   ☐ Easy Effort

Average HR: _____ bpm   Target HR: _____ bpm

Feeling: ☐ Fantastic   ☐ Good   ☐ Difficult   ☐ Very Difficult

Weather:

Temperature: _____°___   Workout Gear: _____

Notes: _____
_____
_____

Friday

Vitals:

Resting HR: _____ bpm   Weight: _____ kg/lbs   Hours Slept: _____ hrs

Sport: _____   **Workout:** _____

Course: _____   Duration: _____   Distance: _____

Intensity: ☐ Max. Effort   ☐ Hard Effort   ☐ Medium Effort   ☐ Easy Effort

Average HR: _____ bpm   Target HR: _____ bpm

Feeling: ☐ Fantastic   ☐ Good   ☐ Difficult   ☐ Very Difficult

Weather:

Temperature: _____°___   Workout Gear: _____

Notes: _____
_____
_____

Week 21   Date: ☐☐☐   Saturday

Vitals:
Resting HR: _____ bpm   Weight: _____ kg/lbs   Hours Slept: _____ hrs

Sport: _____ Workout: _____
Course: _____   Duration: _____   Distance: _____

Intensity: ☐ Max. Effort ☐ Hard Effort ☐ Medium Effort ☐ Easy Effort

Average HR: _____ bpm   Target HR: _____ bpm

Feeling: ☐ Fantastic ☐ Good ☐ Difficult ☐ Very Difficult

Weather:
Temperature: _____°___   Workout Gear: _____

Notes: _____
_____
_____

Week Summary

Total Time: _____ Total Distance: _____

Additional Notes: _____
_____
_____
_____
_____

142

"A race is a work of art that people can look at and
be affected in as many ways as they're capable of
understanding."

— Steve Prefontaine

Vitals:

Resting HR: _____ bpm   Weight: _____ kg/lbs   Hours Slept: _____ hrs

Sport: _____   **Workout:** _____

Course: _____   Duration: _____   Distance: _____

Intensity: ☐ Max. Effort   ☐ Hard Effort   ☐ Medium Effort   ☐ Easy Effort

Average HR: _____ bpm   Target HR: _____ bpm

Feeling: ☐ Fantastic   ☐ Good   ☐ Difficult   ☐ Very Difficult

Weather:

Temperature: _____ ° ___   Workout Gear: _____

Notes: _____

_____

_____

Monday

Vitals:

Resting HR: _____ bpm   Weight: _____ kg/lbs   Hours Slept: _____ hrs

Sport: _____   **Workout:** _____

Course: _____   Duration: _____   Distance: _____

Intensity: ☐ Max. Effort   ☐ Hard Effort   ☐ Medium Effort   ☐ Easy Effort

Average HR: _____ bpm   Target HR: _____ bpm

Feeling: ☐ Fantastic   ☐ Good   ☐ Difficult   ☐ Very Difficult

Weather:

Temperature: _____ ° ___   Workout Gear: _____

Notes: _____

_____

_____

Tuesday

Vitals:

Resting HR: _____ bpm   Weight: _____ kg/lbs   Hours Slept: _____ hrs

Sport: _____   **Workout:** _____

Course: _____   Duration: _____   Distance: _____

Intensity: ☐ Max. Effort   ☐ Hard Effort   ☐ Medium Effort   ☐ Easy Effort

Average HR: _____ bpm   Target HR: _____ bpm

Feeling: ☐ Fantastic   ☐ Good   ☐ Difficult   ☐ Very Difficult

Weather:

Temperature: _____ ° ___   Workout Gear: _____

Notes: _____

_____

_____

Wednesday · Week 22

Vitals:

Resting HR: _____ bpm   Weight: _____ kg/lbs   Hours Slept: _____ hrs

Sport: _____   **Workout:** _____

Course: _____   Duration: _____   Distance: _____

Intensity: ☐ Max. Effort   ☐ Hard Effort   ☐ Medium Effort   ☐ Easy Effort

Average HR: _____ bpm   Target HR: _____ bpm

Feeling: ☐ Fantastic   ☐ Good   ☐ Difficult   ☐ Very Difficult

Weather:

Temperature: _____ ° ___   Workout Gear: _____

Notes: _____
_____
_____

Thursday

Vitals:

Resting HR: _____ bpm   Weight: _____ kg/lbs   Hours Slept: _____ hrs

Sport: _____   **Workout:** _____

Course: _____   Duration: _____   Distance: _____

Intensity: ☐ Max. Effort   ☐ Hard Effort   ☐ Medium Effort   ☐ Easy Effort

Average HR: _____ bpm   Target HR: _____ bpm

Feeling: ☐ Fantastic   ☐ Good   ☐ Difficult   ☐ Very Difficult

Weather:

Temperature: _____ ° ___   Workout Gear: _____

Notes: _____
_____
_____

Friday

Vitals:

Resting HR: _____ bpm   Weight: _____ kg/lbs   Hours Slept: _____ hrs

Sport: _____   **Workout:** _____

Course: _____   Duration: _____   Distance: _____

Intensity: ☐ Max. Effort   ☐ Hard Effort   ☐ Medium Effort   ☐ Easy Effort

Average HR: _____ bpm   Target HR: _____ bpm

Feeling: ☐ Fantastic   ☐ Good   ☐ Difficult   ☐ Very Difficult

Weather:

Temperature: _____ ° ___   Workout Gear: _____

Notes: _____
_____
_____

Vitals:

Resting HR: _____ bpm　　Weight: _____ kg/lbs　Hours Slept: _____ hrs

Sport: _____　**Workout:** _____

Course: _____　　Duration: _____　　Distance: _____

Intensity:　☐ Max. Effort　☐ Hard Effort　☐ Medium Effort　☐ Easy Effort

Average HR: _____ bpm　　Target HR: _____ bpm

Feeling:　☐ Fantastic　☐ Good　☐ Difficult　☐ Very Difficult

Weather:

Temperature: _____ ° ___　　Workout Gear: _____

Notes: _____
_____
_____

Week Summary

Distance / Time

Sunday　Monday　Tuesday　Wednesday　Thursday　Friday　Saturday

Day

Total Time: _____ Total Distance: _____

Additional Notes: _____ _____
_____
_____
_____
_____
_____

Vitals:

Resting HR: _____ bpm   Weight: _____ kg/lbs   Hours Slept: _____ hrs

Sport: _____   **Workout:** _____

Course: _____   Duration: _____   Distance: _____

Intensity: ☐ Max. Effort   ☐ Hard Effort   ☐ Medium Effort   ☐ Easy Effort

Average HR: _____ bpm   Target HR: _____ bpm

Feeling: ☐ Fantastic   ☐ Good   ☐ Difficult   ☐ Very Difficult

Weather:

Temperature: _____ ° ___   Workout Gear: _____

Notes: _____

_____

_____

Monday

Vitals:

Resting HR: _____ bpm   Weight: _____ kg/lbs   Hours Slept: _____ hrs

Sport: _____   **Workout:** _____

Course: _____   Duration: _____   Distance: _____

Intensity: ☐ Max. Effort   ☐ Hard Effort   ☐ Medium Effort   ☐ Easy Effort

Average HR: _____ bpm   Target HR: _____ bpm

Feeling: ☐ Fantastic   ☐ Good   ☐ Difficult   ☐ Very Difficult

Weather:

Temperature: _____ ° ___   Workout Gear: _____

Notes: _____

_____

_____

Tuesday

Vitals:

Resting HR: _____ bpm   Weight: _____ kg/lbs   Hours Slept: _____ hrs

Sport: _____   **Workout:** _____

Course: _____   Duration: _____   Distance: _____

Intensity: ☐ Max. Effort   ☐ Hard Effort   ☐ Medium Effort   ☐ Easy Effort

Average HR: _____ bpm   Target HR: _____ bpm

Feeling: ☐ Fantastic   ☐ Good   ☐ Difficult   ☐ Very Difficult

Weather:

Temperature: _____ ° ___   Workout Gear: _____

Notes: _____

_____

_____

Vitals:

Resting HR: _____ bpm   Weight: _____ kg/lbs   Hours Slept: _____ hrs

Sport: _____   **Workout:** _____

Course: _____   Duration: _____   Distance: _____

Intensity: ☐ Max. Effort   ☐ Hard Effort   ☐ Medium Effort   ☐ Easy Effort

Average HR: _____ bpm   Target HR: _____ bpm

Feeling: ☐ Fantastic   ☐ Good   ☐ Difficult   ☐ Very Difficult

Weather:

Temperature: _____ ° ___   Workout Gear: _____

Notes: _____

_____

_____

Thursday

Vitals:

Resting HR: _____ bpm   Weight: _____ kg/lbs   Hours Slept: _____ hrs

Sport: _____   **Workout:** _____

Course: _____   Duration: _____   Distance: _____

Intensity: ☐ Max. Effort   ☐ Hard Effort   ☐ Medium Effort   ☐ Easy Effort

Average HR: _____ bpm   Target HR: _____ bpm

Feeling: ☐ Fantastic   ☐ Good   ☐ Difficult   ☐ Very Difficult

Weather:

Temperature: _____ ° ___   Workout Gear: _____

Notes: _____

_____

_____

Friday

Vitals:

Resting HR: _____ bpm   Weight: _____ kg/lbs   Hours Slept: _____ hrs

Sport: _____   **Workout:** _____

Course: _____   Duration: _____   Distance: _____

Intensity: ☐ Max. Effort   ☐ Hard Effort   ☐ Medium Effort   ☐ Easy Effort

Average HR: _____ bpm   Target HR: _____ bpm

Feeling: ☐ Fantastic   ☐ Good   ☐ Difficult   ☐ Very Difficult

Weather:

Temperature: _____ ° ___   Workout Gear: _____

Notes: _____

_____

_____

Vitals:

Resting HR: _____ bpm   Weight: _____ kg/lbs   Hours Slept: _____ hrs

Sport: _____   Workout: _____

Course: _____   Duration: _____   Distance: _____

Intensity: ☐ Max. Effort   ☐ Hard Effort   ☐ Medium Effort   ☐ Easy Effort

Average HR: _____ bpm   Target HR: _____ bpm

Feeling: ☐ Fantastic   ☐ Good   ☐ Difficult   ☐ Very Difficult

Weather:

Temperature: _____ ° ___   Workout Gear: _____

Notes: _____

_____

_____

Week Summary

Distance / Time

Sunday   Monday   Tuesday   Wednesday   Thursday   Friday   Saturday

Day

Total Time: _____ Total Distance: _____

Additional Notes: _____

_____

_____

_____

_____

_____

"DO IT AND IT BECOMES A PASSION." JOHN STANTON

Vitals:

Resting HR: _____ bpm   Weight: _____ kg/lbs   Hours Slept: _____ hrs

Sport: _____   **Workout:** _____

Course: _____   Duration: _____   Distance: _____

Intensity: ☐ Max. Effort   ☐ Hard Effort   ☐ Medium Effort   ☐ Easy Effort

Average HR: _____ bpm   Target HR: _____ bpm

Feeling: ☐ Fantastic   ☐ Good   ☐ Difficult   ☐ Very Difficult

Weather:

Temperature: _____ ° ___   Workout Gear: _____

Notes: _____

_____

_____

Vitals:

Resting HR: _____ bpm   Weight: _____ kg/lbs   Hours Slept: _____ hrs

Sport: _____   **Workout:** _____

Course: _____   Duration: _____   Distance: _____

Intensity: ☐ Max. Effort   ☐ Hard Effort   ☐ Medium Effort   ☐ Easy Effort

Average HR: _____ bpm   Target HR: _____ bpm

Feeling: ☐ Fantastic   ☐ Good   ☐ Difficult   ☐ Very Difficult

Weather:

Temperature: _____ ° ___   Workout Gear: _____

Notes: _____

_____

_____

Vitals:

Resting HR: _____ bpm   Weight: _____ kg/lbs   Hours Slept: _____ hrs

Sport: _____   **Workout:** _____

Course: _____   Duration: _____   Distance: _____

Intensity: ☐ Max. Effort   ☐ Hard Effort   ☐ Medium Effort   ☐ Easy Effort

Average HR: _____ bpm   Target HR: _____ bpm

Feeling: ☐ Fantastic   ☐ Good   ☐ Difficult   ☐ Very Difficult

Weather:

Temperature: _____ ° ___   Workout Gear: _____

Notes: _____

_____

_____

Vitals:

Resting HR: _____ bpm   Weight: _____ kg/lbs   Hours Slept: _____ hrs

Sport: _____   **Workout:** _____

Course: _____   Duration: _____   Distance: _____

Intensity: ☐ Max. Effort   ☐ Hard Effort   ☐ Medium Effort   ☐ Easy Effort

Average HR: _____ bpm   Target HR: _____ bpm

Feeling: ☐ Fantastic   ☐ Good   ☐ Difficult   ☐ Very Difficult

Weather:

Temperature: _____ ° ___   Workout Gear: _____

Notes: _____

_____

_____

Thursday

Vitals:

Resting HR: _____ bpm   Weight: _____ kg/lbs   Hours Slept: _____ hrs

Sport: _____   **Workout:** _____

Course: _____   Duration: _____   Distance: _____

Intensity: ☐ Max. Effort   ☐ Hard Effort   ☐ Medium Effort   ☐ Easy Effort

Average HR: _____ bpm   Target HR: _____ bpm

Feeling: ☐ Fantastic   ☐ Good   ☐ Difficult   ☐ Very Difficult

Weather:

Temperature: _____ ° ___   Workout Gear: _____

Notes: _____

_____

_____

Friday

Vitals:

Resting HR: _____ bpm   Weight: _____ kg/lbs   Hours Slept: _____ hrs

Sport: _____   **Workout:** _____

Course: _____   Duration: _____   Distance: _____

Intensity: ☐ Max. Effort   ☐ Hard Effort   ☐ Medium Effort   ☐ Easy Effort

Average HR: _____ bpm   Target HR: _____ bpm

Feeling: ☐ Fantastic   ☐ Good   ☐ Difficult   ☐ Very Difficult

Weather:

Temperature: _____ ° ___   Workout Gear: _____

Notes: _____

_____

_____

Vitals:

Resting HR: _____ bpm   Weight: _____ kg/lbs   Hours Slept: _____ hrs

Sport: _____   **Workout:** _____

Course: _____   Duration: _____   Distance: _____

Intensity: ▢ Max. Effort   ▢ Hard Effort   ▢ Medium Effort   ▢ Easy Effort

Average HR: _____ bpm   Target HR: _____ bpm

Feeling: ▢ Fantastic   ▢ Good   ▢ Difficult   ▢ Very Difficult

Weather:

Temperature: _____°___   Workout Gear: _____

Notes: _____

_____

_____

Week Summary

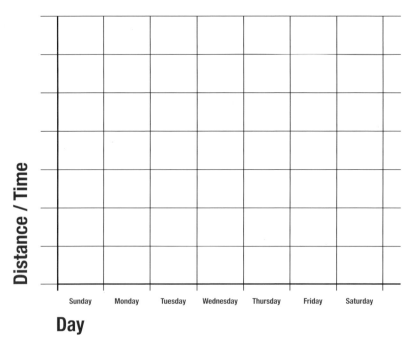

Total Time: _____ Total Distance: _____

Additional Notes: _____

_____

_____

_____

_____

"IT IS A ROUGH ROAD THAT LEADS
TO THE HEIGHTS OF GREATNESS."
-SENECA

Vitals:

Resting HR: _____ bpm   Weight: _____ kg/lbs   Hours Slept: _____ hrs

Sport: _____   **Workout:** _____

Course: _____   Duration: _____   Distance: _____

Intensity: ☐ Max. Effort   ☐ Hard Effort   ☐ Medium Effort   ☐ Easy Effort

Average HR: _____ bpm   Target HR: _____ bpm

Feeling: ☐ Fantastic   ☐ Good   ☐ Difficult   ☐ Very Difficult

Weather:

Temperature: _____ ° ___   Workout Gear: _____

Notes: _____

_____

_____

Vitals:

Resting HR: _____ bpm   Weight: _____ kg/lbs   Hours Slept: _____ hrs

Sport: _____   **Workout:** _____

Course: _____   Duration: _____   Distance: _____

Intensity: ☐ Max. Effort   ☐ Hard Effort   ☐ Medium Effort   ☐ Easy Effort

Average HR: _____ bpm   Target HR: _____ bpm

Feeling: ☐ Fantastic   ☐ Good   ☐ Difficult   ☐ Very Difficult

Weather:

Temperature: _____ ° ___   Workout Gear: _____

Notes: _____

_____

_____

Vitals:

Resting HR: _____ bpm   Weight: _____ kg/lbs   Hours Slept: _____ hrs

Sport: _____   **Workout:** _____

Course: _____   Duration: _____   Distance: _____

Intensity: ☐ Max. Effort   ☐ Hard Effort   ☐ Medium Effort   ☐ Easy Effort

Average HR: _____ bpm   Target HR: _____ bpm

Feeling: ☐ Fantastic   ☐ Good   ☐ Difficult   ☐ Very Difficult

Weather:

Temperature: _____ ° ___   Workout Gear: _____

Notes: _____

_____

_____

Vitals:

Resting HR: _____ bpm   Weight: _____ kg/lbs   Hours Slept: _____ hrs

Sport: _____   **Workout:** _____

Course: _____   Duration: _____   Distance: _____

Intensity: ☐ Max. Effort   ☐ Hard Effort   ☐ Medium Effort   ☐ Easy Effort

Average HR: _____ bpm   Target HR: _____ bpm

Feeling: ☐ Fantastic   ☐ Good   ☐ Difficult   ☐ Very Difficult

Weather:

Temperature: _____ ° ___   Workout Gear: _____

Notes: _____
_____
_____

Thursday

Vitals:

Resting HR: _____ bpm   Weight: _____ kg/lbs   Hours Slept: _____ hrs

Sport: _____   **Workout:** _____

Course: _____   Duration: _____   Distance: _____

Intensity: ☐ Max. Effort   ☐ Hard Effort   ☐ Medium Effort   ☐ Easy Effort

Average HR: _____ bpm   Target HR: _____ bpm

Feeling: ☐ Fantastic   ☐ Good   ☐ Difficult   ☐ Very Difficult

Weather:

Temperature: _____ ° ___   Workout Gear: _____

Notes: _____
_____
_____

Friday

Vitals:

Resting HR: _____ bpm   Weight: _____ kg/lbs   Hours Slept: _____ hrs

Sport: _____   **Workout:** _____

Course: _____   Duration: _____   Distance: _____

Intensity: ☐ Max. Effort   ☐ Hard Effort   ☐ Medium Effort   ☐ Easy Effort

Average HR: _____ bpm   Target HR: _____ bpm

Feeling: ☐ Fantastic   ☐ Good   ☐ Difficult   ☐ Very Difficult

Weather:

Temperature: _____ ° ___   Workout Gear: _____

Notes: _____
_____
_____

Vitals:

Resting HR: _____ bpm   Weight: _____ kg/lbs   Hours Slept: _____ hrs

Sport: _____   Workout: _____

Course: _____   Duration: _____   Distance: _____

Intensity: ☐ Max. Effort ☐ Hard Effort ☐ Medium Effort ☐ Easy Effort

Average HR: _____ bpm   Target HR: _____ bpm

Feeling: ☐ Fantastic   ☐ Good   ☐ Difficult   ☐ Very Difficult

Weather:

Temperature: _____ ° ___   Workout Gear: _____

Notes: _____
_____
_____

Week Summary

Distance / Time

Sunday   Monday   Tuesday   Wednesday   Thursday   Friday   Saturday

Day

Total Time: _____ Total Distance: _____

Additional Notes: _____
_____
_____
_____
_____
_____

"Doubt whom you will,
but never yourself."

~ Christian Bovee

Week 26   Date: ☐ ☐ ☐   Sunday

Vitals:

Resting HR: _____ bpm   Weight: _____ kg/lbs   Hours Slept: _____ hrs

Sport: _____   **Workout:** _____

Course: _____   Duration: _____   Distance: _____

Intensity: ☐ Max. Effort ☐ Hard Effort ☐ Medium Effort ☐ Easy Effort

Average HR: _____ bpm   Target HR: _____ bpm

Feeling: ☐ Fantastic   ☐ Good   ☐ Difficult   ☐ Very Difficult

Weather:

Temperature: _____ ° ___   Workout Gear: _____

Notes: _____

_____

_____

Monday

Vitals:

Resting HR: _____ bpm   Weight: _____ kg/lbs   Hours Slept: _____ hrs

Sport: _____   **Workout:** _____

Course: _____   Duration: _____   Distance: _____

Intensity: ☐ Max. Effort ☐ Hard Effort ☐ Medium Effort ☐ Easy Effort

Average HR: _____ bpm   Target HR: _____ bpm

Feeling: ☐ Fantastic   ☐ Good   ☐ Difficult   ☐ Very Difficult

Weather:

Temperature: _____ ° ___   Workout Gear: _____

Notes: _____

_____

_____

Tuesday

Vitals:

Resting HR: _____ bpm   Weight: _____ kg/lbs   Hours Slept: _____ hrs

Sport: _____   **Workout:** _____

Course: _____   Duration: _____   Distance: _____

Intensity: ☐ Max. Effort ☐ Hard Effort ☐ Medium Effort ☐ Easy Effort

Average HR: _____ bpm   Target HR: _____ bpm

Feeling: ☐ Fantastic   ☐ Good   ☐ Difficult   ☐ Very Difficult

Weather:

Temperature: _____ ° ___   Workout Gear: _____

Notes: _____

_____

_____

Wednesday Week 26

Vitals:

Resting HR: _____ bpm   Weight: _____ kg/lbs   Hours Slept: _____ hrs

Sport: _____   **Workout:** _____

Course: _____   Duration: _____   Distance: _____

Intensity: ☐ Max. Effort ☐ Hard Effort ☐ Medium Effort ☐ Easy Effort

Average HR: _____ bpm   Target HR: _____ bpm

Feeling: ☐ Fantastic ☐ Good ☐ Difficult ☐ Very Difficult

Weather:

Temperature: _____ ° ___   Workout Gear: _____

Notes: _____
_____
_____

Thursday

Vitals:

Resting HR: _____ bpm   Weight: _____ kg/lbs   Hours Slept: _____ hrs

Sport: _____   **Workout:** _____

Course: _____   Duration: _____   Distance: _____

Intensity: ☐ Max. Effort ☐ Hard Effort ☐ Medium Effort ☐ Easy Effort

Average HR: _____ bpm   Target HR: _____ bpm

Feeling: ☐ Fantastic ☐ Good ☐ Difficult ☐ Very Difficult

Weather:

Temperature: _____ ° ___   Workout Gear: _____

Notes: _____
_____
_____

Friday

Vitals:

Resting HR: _____ bpm   Weight: _____ kg/lbs   Hours Slept: _____ hrs

Sport: _____   **Workout:** _____

Course: _____   Duration: _____   Distance: _____

Intensity: ☐ Max. Effort ☐ Hard Effort ☐ Medium Effort ☐ Easy Effort

Average HR: _____ bpm   Target HR: _____ bpm

Feeling: ☐ Fantastic ☐ Good ☐ Difficult ☐ Very Difficult

Weather:

Temperature: _____ ° ___   Workout Gear: _____

Notes: _____
_____
_____

Vitals:

Resting HR: _____ bpm   Weight: _____ kg/lbs   Hours Slept: _____ hrs

Sport: _____   Workout: _____

Course: _____   Duration: _____   Distance: _____

Intensity: ☐ Max. Effort   ☐ Hard Effort   ☐ Medium Effort   ☐ Easy Effort

Average HR: _____ bpm   Target HR: _____ bpm

Feeling: ☐ Fantastic   ☐ Good   ☐ Difficult   ☐ Very Difficult

Weather:

Temperature: _____ ° ___   Workout Gear: _____

Notes: _____
_____
_____

Week Summary

Distance / Time vs **Day** (Sunday, Monday, Tuesday, Wednesday, Thursday, Friday, Saturday)

Total Time: _____ Total Distance: _____

Additional Notes: _____
_____
_____
_____
_____

"ARRIVING AT ONE GOAL IS THE STARTING POINT TO ANOTHER."
~ JOHN DEWEY

Vitals:

Resting HR: _____ bpm   Weight: _____ kg/lbs   Hours Slept: _____ hrs

Sport: _____   **Workout:** _____

Course: _____   Duration: _____   Distance: _____

Intensity: ☐ Max. Effort ☐ Hard Effort ☐ Medium Effort ☐ Easy Effort

Average HR: _____ bpm   Target HR: _____ bpm

Feeling: ☐ Fantastic ☐ Good ☐ Difficult ☐ Very Difficult

Weather:

Temperature: _____ ° ___   Workout Gear: _____

Notes: _____
_____
_____

Monday

Vitals:

Resting HR: _____ bpm   Weight: _____ kg/lbs   Hours Slept: _____ hrs

Sport: _____   **Workout:** _____

Course: _____   Duration: _____   Distance: _____

Intensity: ☐ Max. Effort ☐ Hard Effort ☐ Medium Effort ☐ Easy Effort

Average HR: _____ bpm   Target HR: _____ bpm

Feeling: ☐ Fantastic ☐ Good ☐ Difficult ☐ Very Difficult

Weather:

Temperature: _____ ° ___   Workout Gear: _____

Notes: _____
_____
_____

Tuesday

Vitals:

Resting HR: _____ bpm   Weight: _____ kg/lbs   Hours Slept: _____ hrs

Sport: _____   **Workout:** _____

Course: _____   Duration: _____   Distance: _____

Intensity: ☐ Max. Effort ☐ Hard Effort ☐ Medium Effort ☐ Easy Effort

Average HR: _____ bpm   Target HR: _____ bpm

Feeling: ☐ Fantastic ☐ Good ☐ Difficult ☐ Very Difficult

Weather:

Temperature: _____ ° ___   Workout Gear: _____

Notes: _____
_____
_____

Wednesday Week 27

Vitals:

Resting HR: _____ bpm   Weight: _____ kg/lbs   Hours Slept: _____ hrs

Sport: _____   **Workout:** _____

Course: _____   Duration: _____   Distance: _____

Intensity: ☐ Max. Effort   ☐ Hard Effort   ☐ Medium Effort   ☐ Easy Effort

Average HR: _____ bpm   Target HR: _____ bpm

Feeling: ☐ Fantastic   ☐ Good   ☐ Difficult   ☐ Very Difficult

Weather:

Temperature: _____ ° ___   Workout Gear: _____

Notes: _____

_____

_____

Thursday

Vitals:

Resting HR: _____ bpm   Weight: _____ kg/lbs   Hours Slept: _____ hrs

Sport: _____   **Workout:** _____

Course: _____   Duration: _____   Distance: _____

Intensity: ☐ Max. Effort   ☐ Hard Effort   ☐ Medium Effort   ☐ Easy Effort

Average HR: _____ bpm   Target HR: _____ bpm

Feeling: ☐ Fantastic   ☐ Good   ☐ Difficult   ☐ Very Difficult

Weather:

Temperature: _____ ° ___   Workout Gear: _____

Notes: _____

_____

_____

Friday

Vitals:

Resting HR: _____ bpm   Weight: _____ kg/lbs   Hours Slept: _____ hrs

Sport: _____   **Workout:** _____

Course: _____   Duration: _____   Distance: _____

Intensity: ☐ Max. Effort   ☐ Hard Effort   ☐ Medium Effort   ☐ Easy Effort

Average HR: _____ bpm   Target HR: _____ bpm

Feeling: ☐ Fantastic   ☐ Good   ☐ Difficult   ☐ Very Difficult

Weather:

Temperature: _____ ° ___   Workout Gear: _____

Notes: _____

_____

_____

Vitals:

Resting HR: _____ bpm　　Weight: _____ kg/lbs　Hours Slept: _____ hrs

Sport: _____　**Workout:** _____

Course: _____　Duration: _____　Distance: _____

Intensity:　☐ Max. Effort　☐ Hard Effort　☐ Medium Effort　☐ Easy Effort

Average HR: _____ bpm　　Target HR: _____ bpm

Feeling:　☐ Fantastic　☐ Good　☐ Difficult　☐ Very Difficult

Weather:

Temperature: _____ ° ___　　Workout Gear: _____

Notes: _____

_____

_____

Week Summary

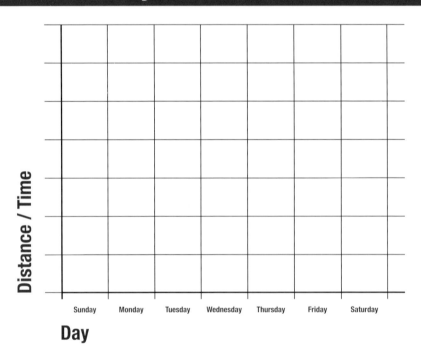

Total Time: _____ Total Distance: _____

Additional Notes: _____

_____

_____

_____

_____

_____

" All we need to make us really happy
is something to be enthusiastic about. "
– Charles Kingsley

Vitals:

Resting HR: _____ bpm   Weight: _____ kg/lbs   Hours Slept: _____ hrs

Sport: _____   **Workout:** _____

Course: _____   Duration: _____   Distance: _____

Intensity: ☐ Max. Effort   ☐ Hard Effort   ☐ Medium Effort   ☐ Easy Effort

Average HR: _____ bpm   Target HR: _____ bpm

Feeling: ☐ Fantastic   ☐ Good   ☐ Difficult   ☐ Very Difficult

Weather:

Temperature: _____ ° ___   Workout Gear: _____

Notes: _____

_____

_____

Monday

Vitals:

Resting HR: _____ bpm   Weight: _____ kg/lbs   Hours Slept: _____ hrs

Sport: _____   **Workout:** _____

Course: _____   Duration: _____   Distance: _____

Intensity: ☐ Max. Effort   ☐ Hard Effort   ☐ Medium Effort   ☐ Easy Effort

Average HR: _____ bpm   Target HR: _____ bpm

Feeling: ☐ Fantastic   ☐ Good   ☐ Difficult   ☐ Very Difficult

Weather:

Temperature: _____ ° ___   Workout Gear: _____

Notes: _____

_____

_____

Tuesday

Vitals:

Resting HR: _____ bpm   Weight: _____ kg/lbs   Hours Slept: _____ hrs

Sport: _____   **Workout:** _____

Course: _____   Duration: _____   Distance: _____

Intensity: ☐ Max. Effort   ☐ Hard Effort   ☐ Medium Effort   ☐ Easy Effort

Average HR: _____ bpm   Target HR: _____ bpm

Feeling: ☐ Fantastic   ☐ Good   ☐ Difficult   ☐ Very Difficult

Weather:

Temperature: _____ ° ___   Workout Gear: _____

Notes: _____

_____

_____

Vitals:

Resting HR: _____ bpm   Weight: _____ kg/lbs   Hours Slept: _____ hrs

Sport: _____   **Workout:** _____

Course: _____   Duration: _____   Distance: _____

Intensity: ☐ Max. Effort   ☐ Hard Effort   ☐ Medium Effort   ☐ Easy Effort

Average HR: _____ bpm   Target HR: _____ bpm

Feeling: ☐ Fantastic   ☐ Good   ☐ Difficult   ☐ Very Difficult

Weather:

Temperature: _____ ° ___   Workout Gear: _____

Notes: _____
_____
_____

Thursday

Vitals:

Resting HR: _____ bpm   Weight: _____ kg/lbs   Hours Slept: _____ hrs

Sport: _____   **Workout:** _____

Course: _____   Duration: _____   Distance: _____

Intensity: ☐ Max. Effort   ☐ Hard Effort   ☐ Medium Effort   ☐ Easy Effort

Average HR: _____ bpm   Target HR: _____ bpm

Feeling: ☐ Fantastic   ☐ Good   ☐ Difficult   ☐ Very Difficult

Weather:

Temperature: _____ ° ___   Workout Gear: _____

Notes: _____
_____
_____

Friday

Vitals:

Resting HR: _____ bpm   Weight: _____ kg/lbs   Hours Slept: _____ hrs

Sport: _____   **Workout:** _____

Course: _____   Duration: _____   Distance: _____

Intensity: ☐ Max. Effort   ☐ Hard Effort   ☐ Medium Effort   ☐ Easy Effort

Average HR: _____ bpm   Target HR: _____ bpm

Feeling: ☐ Fantastic   ☐ Good   ☐ Difficult   ☐ Very Difficult

Weather:

Temperature: _____ ° ___   Workout Gear: _____

Notes: _____
_____
_____

Vitals:

Resting HR: _____ bpm   Weight: _____ kg/lbs   Hours Slept: _____ hrs

Sport: _____   **Workout:** _____

Course: _____   Duration: _____   Distance: _____

Intensity: ☐ Max. Effort   ☐ Hard Effort   ☐ Medium Effort   ☐ Easy Effort

Average HR: _____ bpm   Target HR: _____ bpm

Feeling: ☐ Fantastic   ☐ Good   ☐ Difficult   ☐ Very Difficult

Weather:

Temperature: _____ ° ___   Workout Gear: _____

Notes: _____
_____
_____

Week Summary

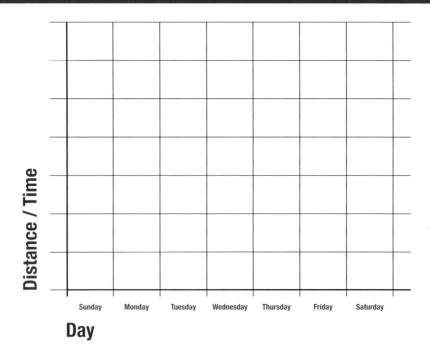

Total Time: _____ Total Distance: _____

Additional Notes: _____
_____
_____
_____
_____

THON
TAWA
FINISH
2:32.19
TAWA CITIZEN
ING
OTTAWA
MARATHON
ING
ING
ING
"Everyone in life is looking for a certain rush. Racing is where I get mine."
~John Trautmann

Vitals:

Resting HR: _____ bpm   Weight: _____ kg/lbs   Hours Slept: _____ hrs

Sport: _____   **Workout:** _____

Course: _____   Duration: _____   Distance: _____

Intensity: ☐ Max. Effort   ☐ Hard Effort   ☐ Medium Effort   ☐ Easy Effort

Average HR: _____ bpm   Target HR: _____ bpm

Feeling: ☐ Fantastic   ☐ Good   ☐ Difficult   ☐ Very Difficult

Weather:

Temperature: _____°___   Workout Gear: _____

Notes: _____

_____

_____

Monday

Vitals:

Resting HR: _____ bpm   Weight: _____ kg/lbs   Hours Slept: _____ hrs

Sport: _____   **Workout:** _____

Course: _____   Duration: _____   Distance: _____

Intensity: ☐ Max. Effort   ☐ Hard Effort   ☐ Medium Effort   ☐ Easy Effort

Average HR: _____ bpm   Target HR: _____ bpm

Feeling: ☐ Fantastic   ☐ Good   ☐ Difficult   ☐ Very Difficult

Weather:

Temperature: _____°___   Workout Gear: _____

Notes: _____

_____

_____

Tuesday

Vitals:

Resting HR: _____ bpm   Weight: _____ kg/lbs   Hours Slept: _____ hrs

Sport: _____   **Workout:** _____

Course: _____   Duration: _____   Distance: _____

Intensity: ☐ Max. Effort   ☐ Hard Effort   ☐ Medium Effort   ☐ Easy Effort

Average HR: _____ bpm   Target HR: _____ bpm

Feeling: ☐ Fantastic   ☐ Good   ☐ Difficult   ☐ Very Difficult

Weather:

Temperature: _____°___   Workout Gear: _____

Notes: _____

_____

_____

Vitals:

Resting HR: _____ bpm   Weight: _____ kg/lbs   Hours Slept: _____ hrs

Sport: _____   **Workout:** _____

Course: _____   Duration: _____   Distance: _____

Intensity: ☐ Max. Effort ☐ Hard Effort ☐ Medium Effort ☐ Easy Effort

Average HR: _____ bpm   Target HR: _____ bpm

Feeling: ☐ Fantastic ☐ Good ☐ Difficult ☐ Very Difficult

Weather:

Temperature: _____ ° ___   Workout Gear: _____

Notes: _____

_____

_____

Thursday

Vitals:

Resting HR: _____ bpm   Weight: _____ kg/lbs   Hours Slept: _____ hrs

Sport: _____   **Workout:** _____

Course: _____   Duration: _____   Distance: _____

Intensity: ☐ Max. Effort ☐ Hard Effort ☐ Medium Effort ☐ Easy Effort

Average HR: _____ bpm   Target HR: _____ bpm

Feeling: ☐ Fantastic ☐ Good ☐ Difficult ☐ Very Difficult

Weather:

Temperature: _____ ° ___   Workout Gear: _____

Notes: _____

_____

_____

Friday

Vitals:

Resting HR: _____ bpm   Weight: _____ kg/lbs   Hours Slept: _____ hrs

Sport: _____   **Workout:** _____

Course: _____   Duration: _____   Distance: _____

Intensity: ☐ Max. Effort ☐ Hard Effort ☐ Medium Effort ☐ Easy Effort

Average HR: _____ bpm   Target HR: _____ bpm

Feeling: ☐ Fantastic ☐ Good ☐ Difficult ☐ Very Difficult

Weather:

Temperature: _____ ° ___   Workout Gear: _____

Notes: _____

_____

_____

Vitals:

Resting HR: _____ bpm   Weight: _____ kg/lbs   Hours Slept: _____ hrs

Sport: _____   Workout: _____

Course: _____   Duration: _____   Distance: _____

Intensity: ☐ Max. Effort   ☐ Hard Effort   ☐ Medium Effort   ☐ Easy Effort

Average HR: _____ bpm   Target HR: _____ bpm

Feeling: ☐ Fantastic   ☐ Good   ☐ Difficult   ☐ Very Difficult

Weather:

Temperature: _____ ° ___   Workout Gear: _____

Notes: _____

_____

_____

Week Summary

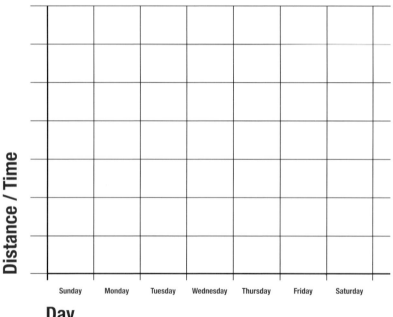

Total Time: _____ Total Distance: _____

Additional Notes: _____

_____

_____

_____

_____

"GREAT THINGS ARE NOT DONE BY IMPULSE BUT BY A SERIES OF SMALL THINGS BROUGHT TOGETHER" — VINCENT VAN GOGH

Vitals:

Resting HR: _____ bpm   Weight: _____ kg/lbs   Hours Slept: _____ hrs

Sport: _____   **Workout:** _____

Course: _____   Duration: _____   Distance: _____

Intensity: □ Max. Effort   □ Hard Effort   □ Medium Effort   □ Easy Effort

Average HR: _____ bpm   Target HR: _____ bpm

Feeling: □ Fantastic   □ Good   □ Difficult   □ Very Difficult

Weather:

Temperature: _____ ° ___   Workout Gear: _____

Notes: _____
_____
_____

Monday

Vitals:

Resting HR: _____ bpm   Weight: _____ kg/lbs   Hours Slept: _____ hrs

Sport: _____   **Workout:** _____

Course: _____   Duration: _____   Distance: _____

Intensity: □ Max. Effort   □ Hard Effort   □ Medium Effort   □ Easy Effort

Average HR: _____ bpm   Target HR: _____ bpm

Feeling: □ Fantastic   □ Good   □ Difficult   □ Very Difficult

Weather:

Temperature: _____ ° ___   Workout Gear: _____

Notes: _____
_____
_____

Tuesday

Vitals:

Resting HR: _____ bpm   Weight: _____ kg/lbs   Hours Slept: _____ hrs

Sport: _____   **Workout:** _____

Course: _____   Duration: _____   Distance: _____

Intensity: □ Max. Effort   □ Hard Effort   □ Medium Effort   □ Easy Effort

Average HR: _____ bpm   Target HR: _____ bpm

Feeling: □ Fantastic   □ Good   □ Difficult   □ Very Difficult

Weather:

Temperature: _____ ° ___   Workout Gear: _____

Notes: _____
_____
_____

Vitals:

Resting HR: _____ bpm   Weight: _____ kg/lbs   Hours Slept: _____ hrs

Sport: _____   **Workout:** _____

Course: _____   Duration: _____   Distance: _____

Intensity: ☐ Max. Effort   ☐ Hard Effort   ☐ Medium Effort   ☐ Easy Effort

Average HR: _____ bpm   Target HR: _____ bpm

Feeling: ☐ Fantastic   ☐ Good   ☐ Difficult   ☐ Very Difficult

Weather:

Temperature: _____ ° ___   Workout Gear: _____

Notes: _____

_____

_____

Thursday

Vitals:

Resting HR: _____ bpm   Weight: _____ kg/lbs   Hours Slept: _____ hrs

Sport: _____   **Workout:**_____

Course: _____   Duration: _____   Distance: _____

Intensity: ☐ Max. Effort   ☐ Hard Effort   ☐ Medium Effort   ☐ Easy Effort

Average HR: _____ bpm   Target HR: _____ bpm

Feeling: ☐ Fantastic   ☐ Good   ☐ Difficult   ☐ Very Difficult

Weather:

Temperature: _____ ° ___   Workout Gear: _____

Notes: _____

_____

_____

Friday

Vitals:

Resting HR: _____ bpm   Weight: _____ kg/lbs   Hours Slept: _____ hrs

Sport: _____   **Workout:**_____

Course: _____   Duration: _____   Distance: _____

Intensity: ☐ Max. Effort   ☐ Hard Effort   ☐ Medium Effort   ☐ Easy Effort

Average HR: _____ bpm   Target HR: _____ bpm

Feeling: ☐ Fantastic   ☐ Good   ☐ Difficult   ☐ Very Difficult

Weather:

Temperature: _____ ° ___   Workout Gear: _____

Notes: _____

_____

_____

Vitals:

Resting HR: _____ bpm   Weight: _____ kg/lbs   Hours Slept: _____ hrs

Sport: _____   Workout: _____

Course: _____   Duration: _____   Distance: _____

Intensity: ☐ Max. Effort   ☐ Hard Effort   ☐ Medium Effort   ☐ Easy Effort

Average HR: _____ bpm   Target HR: _____ bpm

Feeling: ☐ Fantastic   ☐ Good   ☐ Difficult   ☐ Very Difficult

Weather:

Temperature: _____ ° ___   Workout Gear: _____

Notes: _____
_____
_____

Week Summary

Total Time: _____ Total Distance: _____

Additional Notes: _____
_____
_____
_____
_____
_____

"RUNNING IS THE GREATEST
METAPHOR FOR LIFE BECAUSE
YOU GET OUT OF IT
WHAT YOU PUT INTO IT."
—OPRAH WINFREY

Vitals:

Resting HR: _____ bpm   Weight: _____ kg/lbs   Hours Slept: _____ hrs

Sport: _____   **Workout:** _____

Course: _____   Duration: _____   Distance: _____

Intensity: ☐ Max. Effort   ☐ Hard Effort   ☐ Medium Effort   ☐ Easy Effort

Average HR: _____ bpm   Target HR: _____ bpm

Feeling: ☐ Fantastic   ☐ Good   ☐ Difficult   ☐ Very Difficult

Weather:

Temperature: _____ ° ___   Workout Gear: _____

Notes: _____

_____

_____

Vitals:

Resting HR: _____ bpm   Weight: _____ kg/lbs   Hours Slept: _____ hrs

Sport: _____   **Workout:** _____

Course: _____   Duration: _____   Distance: _____

Intensity: ☐ Max. Effort   ☐ Hard Effort   ☐ Medium Effort   ☐ Easy Effort

Average HR: _____ bpm   Target HR: _____ bpm

Feeling: ☐ Fantastic   ☐ Good   ☐ Difficult   ☐ Very Difficult

Weather:

Temperature: _____ ° ___   Workout Gear: _____

Notes: _____

_____

_____

Vitals:

Resting HR: _____ bpm   Weight: _____ kg/lbs   Hours Slept: _____ hrs

Sport: _____   **Workout:** _____

Course: _____   Duration: _____   Distance: _____

Intensity: ☐ Max. Effort   ☐ Hard Effort   ☐ Medium Effort   ☐ Easy Effort

Average HR: _____ bpm   Target HR: _____ bpm

Feeling: ☐ Fantastic   ☐ Good   ☐ Difficult   ☐ Very Difficult

Weather:

Temperature: _____ ° ___   Workout Gear: _____

Notes: _____

_____

_____

Vitals:

Resting HR: _____ bpm　　Weight: _____ kg/lbs　Hours Slept: _____ hrs

Sport: _____　**Workout:** _____

Course: _____　　Duration: _____　　Distance: _____

Intensity:　□ Max. Effort　□ Hard Effort　□ Medium Effort　□ Easy Effort

Average HR: _____ bpm　　　Target HR: _____ bpm

Feeling:　□ Fantastic　　□ Good　　□ Difficult　　□ Very Difficult

Weather:

Temperature: _____ ° ___　　Workout Gear: _____

Notes: _____

_____

_____

Thursday

Vitals:

Resting HR: _____ bpm　　Weight: _____ kg/lbs　Hours Slept: _____ hrs

Sport: _____　**Workout:** _____

Course: _____　　Duration: _____　　Distance: _____

Intensity:　□ Max. Effort　□ Hard Effort　□ Medium Effort　□ Easy Effort

Average HR: _____ bpm　　　Target HR: _____ bpm

Feeling:　□ Fantastic　　□ Good　　□ Difficult　　□ Very Difficult

Weather:

Temperature: _____ ° ___　　Workout Gear: _____

Notes: _____

_____

_____

Friday

Vitals:

Resting HR: _____ bpm　　Weight: _____ kg/lbs　Hours Slept: _____ hrs

Sport: _____　**Workout:** _____

Course: _____　　Duration: _____　　Distance: _____

Intensity:　□ Max. Effort　□ Hard Effort　□ Medium Effort　□ Easy Effort

Average HR: _____ bpm　　　Target HR: _____ bpm

Feeling:　□ Fantastic　　□ Good　　□ Difficult　　□ Very Difficult

Weather:

Temperature: _____ ° ___　　Workout Gear: _____

Notes: _____

_____

_____

Vitals:

Resting HR: _____ bpm　　Weight: _____ kg/lbs　　Hours Slept: _____ hrs

Sport: _____　**Workout:** _____

Course: _____　　Duration: _____　　Distance: _____

Intensity:　☐ Max. Effort　☐ Hard Effort　☐ Medium Effort　☐ Easy Effort

Average HR: _____ bpm　　Target HR: _____ bpm

Feeling:　☐ Fantastic　☐ Good　☐ Difficult　☐ Very Difficult

Weather:

Temperature: _____ ° ___　　Workout Gear: _____

Notes: _____

_____

_____

Week Summary

Day

Total Time: _____ Total Distance: _____

Additional Notes: _____

_____
_____
_____
_____
_____

"TRUE SPORT IS ALWAYS A DUEL: A DUEL WITH NATURE, WITH ONE'S OWN FEAR, WITH ONE'S OWN FATIGUE, A DUEL IN WHICH BODY AND MIND ARE STRENGTHENED."
–YEVGENY YEVTUSHENKO, RUSSIAN POET

Vitals:

Resting HR: _____ bpm   Weight: _____ kg/lbs   Hours Slept: _____ hrs

Sport: _____   **Workout:** _____

Course: _____   Duration: _____   Distance: _____

Intensity: ☐ Max. Effort   ☐ Hard Effort   ☐ Medium Effort   ☐ Easy Effort

Average HR: _____ bpm   Target HR: _____ bpm

Feeling: ☐ Fantastic   ☐ Good   ☐ Difficult   ☐ Very Difficult

Weather:

Temperature: _____ ° ___   Workout Gear: _____

Notes: _____
_____
_____

Vitals:

Resting HR: _____ bpm   Weight: _____ kg/lbs   Hours Slept: _____ hrs

Sport: _____   **Workout:** _____

Course: _____   Duration: _____   Distance: _____

Intensity: ☐ Max. Effort   ☐ Hard Effort   ☐ Medium Effort   ☐ Easy Effort

Average HR: _____ bpm   Target HR: _____ bpm

Feeling: ☐ Fantastic   ☐ Good   ☐ Difficult   ☐ Very Difficult

Weather:

Temperature: _____ ° ___   Workout Gear: _____

Notes: _____
_____
_____

Vitals:

Resting HR: _____ bpm   Weight: _____ kg/lbs   Hours Slept: _____ hrs

Sport: _____   **Workout:** _____

Course: _____   Duration: _____   Distance: _____

Intensity: ☐ Max. Effort   ☐ Hard Effort   ☐ Medium Effort   ☐ Easy Effort

Average HR: _____ bpm   Target HR: _____ bpm

Feeling: ☐ Fantastic   ☐ Good   ☐ Difficult   ☐ Very Difficult

Weather:

Temperature: _____ ° ___   Workout Gear: _____

Notes: _____
_____
_____

Vitals:

Resting HR: _____ bpm   Weight: _____ kg/lbs   Hours Slept: _____ hrs

Sport: _____   **Workout:** _____

Course: _____   Duration: _____   Distance: _____

Intensity: □ Max. Effort   □ Hard Effort   □ Medium Effort   □ Easy Effort

Average HR: _____ bpm   Target HR: _____ bpm

Feeling: □ Fantastic   □ Good   □ Difficult   □ Very Difficult

Weather:

Temperature: _____ ° ___   Workout Gear: _____

Notes: _____
_____
_____

Vitals:

Resting HR: _____ bpm   Weight: _____ kg/lbs   Hours Slept: _____ hrs

Sport: _____   **Workout:** _____

Course: _____   Duration: _____   Distance: _____

Intensity: □ Max. Effort   □ Hard Effort   □ Medium Effort   □ Easy Effort

Average HR: _____ bpm   Target HR: _____ bpm

Feeling: □ Fantastic   □ Good   □ Difficult   □ Very Difficult

Weather:

Temperature: _____ ° ___   Workout Gear: _____

Notes: _____
_____
_____

Vitals:

Resting HR: _____ bpm   Weight: _____ kg/lbs   Hours Slept: _____ hrs

Sport: _____   **Workout:** _____

Course: _____   Duration: _____   Distance: _____

Intensity: □ Max. Effort   □ Hard Effort   □ Medium Effort   □ Easy Effort

Average HR: _____ bpm   Target HR: _____ bpm

Feeling: □ Fantastic   □ Good   □ Difficult   □ Very Difficult

Weather:

Temperature: _____ ° ___   Workout Gear: _____

Notes: _____
_____
_____

Vitals:

Resting HR: _____ bpm   Weight: _____ kg/lbs   Hours Slept: _____ hrs

Sport: _____   Workout: _____

Course: _____   Duration: _____   Distance: _____

Intensity: ☐ Max. Effort   ☐ Hard Effort   ☐ Medium Effort   ☐ Easy Effort

Average HR: _____ bpm   Target HR: _____ bpm

Feeling: ☐ Fantastic   ☐ Good   ☐ Difficult   ☐ Very Difficult

Weather:

Temperature: _____ ° ___   Workout Gear: _____

Notes: _____

_____

_____

Week Summary

Total Time: _____ Total Distance: _____

Additional Notes: _____

_____

_____

_____

_____

_____

"WORKOUTS ARE LIKE BRUSHING MY TEETH; I DON'T THINK ABOUT THEM, I JUST DO THEM. THE DECISION HAS ALREADY BEEN MADE." — PATTI SUE PLUMER, U.S. OLYMPIAN

Vitals:

Resting HR: _____ bpm   Weight: _____ kg/lbs   Hours Slept: _____ hrs

Sport: _____   **Workout:** _____

Course: _____   Duration: _____   Distance: _____

Intensity: ☐ Max. Effort ☐ Hard Effort ☐ Medium Effort ☐ Easy Effort

Average HR: _____ bpm   Target HR: _____ bpm

Feeling: ☐ Fantastic ☐ Good ☐ Difficult ☐ Very Difficult

Weather:

Temperature: _____ ° ___   Workout Gear: _____

Notes: _____

_____

_____

Vitals:

Resting HR: _____ bpm   Weight: _____ kg/lbs   Hours Slept: _____ hrs

Sport: _____   **Workout:** _____

Course: _____   Duration: _____   Distance: _____

Intensity: ☐ Max. Effort ☐ Hard Effort ☐ Medium Effort ☐ Easy Effort

Average HR: _____ bpm   Target HR: _____ bpm

Feeling: ☐ Fantastic ☐ Good ☐ Difficult ☐ Very Difficult

Weather:

Temperature: _____ ° ___   Workout Gear: _____

Notes: _____

_____

_____

Vitals:

Resting HR: _____ bpm   Weight: _____ kg/lbs   Hours Slept: _____ hrs

Sport: _____   **Workout:** _____

Course: _____   Duration: _____   Distance: _____

Intensity: ☐ Max. Effort ☐ Hard Effort ☐ Medium Effort ☐ Easy Effort

Average HR: _____ bpm   Target HR: _____ bpm

Feeling: ☐ Fantastic ☐ Good ☐ Difficult ☐ Very Difficult

Weather:

Temperature: _____ ° ___   Workout Gear: _____

Notes: _____

_____

_____

Vitals:

Resting HR: _____ bpm   Weight: _____ kg/lbs   Hours Slept: _____ hrs

Sport: _____   **Workout:** _____

Course: _____   Duration: _____   Distance: _____

Intensity: ☐ Max. Effort   ☐ Hard Effort   ☐ Medium Effort   ☐ Easy Effort

Average HR: _____ bpm   Target HR: _____ bpm

Feeling: ☐ Fantastic   ☐ Good   ☐ Difficult   ☐ Very Difficult

Weather:

Temperature: _____ ° ___   Workout Gear: _____

Notes: _____

_____

_____

Thursday

Vitals:

Resting HR: _____ bpm   Weight: _____ kg/lbs   Hours Slept: _____ hrs

Sport: _____   **Workout:** _____

Course: _____   Duration: _____   Distance: _____

Intensity: ☐ Max. Effort   ☐ Hard Effort   ☐ Medium Effort   ☐ Easy Effort

Average HR: _____ bpm   Target HR: _____ bpm

Feeling: ☐ Fantastic   ☐ Good   ☐ Difficult   ☐ Very Difficult

Weather:

Temperature: _____ ° ___   Workout Gear: _____

Notes: _____

_____

_____

Friday

Vitals:

Resting HR: _____ bpm   Weight: _____ kg/lbs   Hours Slept: _____ hrs

Sport: _____   **Workout:** _____

Course: _____   Duration: _____   Distance: _____

Intensity: ☐ Max. Effort   ☐ Hard Effort   ☐ Medium Effort   ☐ Easy Effort

Average HR: _____ bpm   Target HR: _____ bpm

Feeling: ☐ Fantastic   ☐ Good   ☐ Difficult   ☐ Very Difficult

Weather:

Temperature: _____ ° ___   Workout Gear: _____

Notes: _____

_____

_____

Vitals:

Resting HR: _____ bpm   Weight: _____ kg/lbs   Hours Slept: _____ hrs

Sport: _____   Workout: _____

Course: _____   Duration: _____   Distance: _____

Intensity: ☐ Max. Effort   ☐ Hard Effort   ☐ Medium Effort   ☐ Easy Effort

Average HR: _____ bpm   Target HR: _____ bpm

Feeling: ☐ Fantastic   ☐ Good   ☐ Difficult   ☐ Very Difficult

Weather:

Temperature: _____ ° ___   Workout Gear: _____

Notes: _____

_____

_____

Week Summary

Total Time: _____ Total Distance: _____

Additional Notes: _____

_____

_____

_____

_____

_____

"Our greatest glory consists not in never falling, but in rising every time we fall."
-Ralph Waldo Emerson

Vitals:

Resting HR: _____ bpm   Weight: _____ kg/lbs   Hours Slept: _____ hrs

Sport: _____   **Workout:** _____

Course: _____   Duration: _____   Distance: _____

Intensity: ☐ Max. Effort   ☐ Hard Effort   ☐ Medium Effort   ☐ Easy Effort

Average HR: _____ bpm   Target HR: _____ bpm

Feeling: ☐ Fantastic   ☐ Good   ☐ Difficult   ☐ Very Difficult

Weather:

Temperature: _____ ° ___   Workout Gear: _____

Notes: _____

_____

_____

Monday

Vitals:

Resting HR: _____ bpm   Weight: _____ kg/lbs   Hours Slept: _____ hrs

Sport: _____   **Workout:** _____

Course: _____   Duration: _____   Distance: _____

Intensity: ☐ Max. Effort   ☐ Hard Effort   ☐ Medium Effort   ☐ Easy Effort

Average HR: _____ bpm   Target HR: _____ bpm

Feeling: ☐ Fantastic   ☐ Good   ☐ Difficult   ☐ Very Difficult

Weather:

Temperature: _____ ° ___   Workout Gear: _____

Notes: _____

_____

_____

Tuesday

Vitals:

Resting HR: _____ bpm   Weight: _____ kg/lbs   Hours Slept: _____ hrs

Sport: _____   **Workout:** _____

Course: _____   Duration: _____   Distance: _____

Intensity: ☐ Max. Effort   ☐ Hard Effort   ☐ Medium Effort   ☐ Easy Effort

Average HR: _____ bpm   Target HR: _____ bpm

Feeling: ☐ Fantastic   ☐ Good   ☐ Difficult   ☐ Very Difficult

Weather:

Temperature: _____ ° ___   Workout Gear: _____

Notes: _____

_____

_____

Wednesday Week 34

Vitals:

Resting HR: _____ bpm   Weight: _____ kg/lbs   Hours Slept: _____ hrs

Sport: _____ **Workout:** _____

Course: _____   Duration: _____   Distance: _____

Intensity: ☐ Max. Effort   ☐ Hard Effort   ☐ Medium Effort   ☐ Easy Effort

Average HR: _____ bpm   Target HR: _____ bpm

Feeling: ☐ Fantastic   ☐ Good   ☐ Difficult   ☐ Very Difficult

Weather:

Temperature: _____ ° ___   Workout Gear: _____

Notes: _____

_____

_____

Thursday

Vitals:

Resting HR: _____ bpm   Weight: _____ kg/lbs   Hours Slept: _____ hrs

Sport: _____ **Workout:** _____

Course: _____   Duration: _____   Distance: _____

Intensity: ☐ Max. Effort   ☐ Hard Effort   ☐ Medium Effort   ☐ Easy Effort

Average HR: _____ bpm   Target HR: _____ bpm

Feeling: ☐ Fantastic   ☐ Good   ☐ Difficult   ☐ Very Difficult

Weather:

Temperature: _____ ° ___   Workout Gear: _____

Notes: _____

_____

_____

Friday

Vitals:

Resting HR: _____ bpm   Weight: _____ kg/lbs   Hours Slept: _____ hrs

Sport: _____ **Workout:** _____

Course: _____   Duration: _____   Distance: _____

Intensity: ☐ Max. Effort   ☐ Hard Effort   ☐ Medium Effort   ☐ Easy Effort

Average HR: _____ bpm   Target HR: _____ bpm

Feeling: ☐ Fantastic   ☐ Good   ☐ Difficult   ☐ Very Difficult

Weather:

Temperature: _____ ° ___   Workout Gear: _____

Notes: _____

_____

_____

Vitals:

Resting HR: _____ bpm   Weight: _____ kg/lbs   Hours Slept: _____ hrs

Sport: _____   Workout: _____

Course: _____   Duration: _____   Distance: _____

Intensity: ☐ Max. Effort   ☐ Hard Effort   ☐ Medium Effort   ☐ Easy Effort

Average HR: _____ bpm   Target HR: _____ bpm

Feeling: ☐ Fantastic   ☐ Good   ☐ Difficult   ☐ Very Difficult

Weather:

Temperature: _____ ° ___   Workout Gear: _____

Notes: _____

_____

_____

Week Summary

Distance / Time

Sunday   Monday   Tuesday   Wednesday   Thursday   Friday   Saturday

Day

Total Time: _____ Total Distance: _____

Additional Notes: _____

_____

_____

_____

_____

_____

194

"To describe the agony of a marathon to someone who has never run it is like trying to explain color to someone who was born blind."

— Jerome Drayton

Vitals:

Resting HR: _____ bpm   Weight: _____ kg/lbs   Hours Slept: _____ hrs

Sport: _____   **Workout:** _____

Course: _____   Duration: _____   Distance: _____

Intensity: ☐ Max. Effort   ☐ Hard Effort   ☐ Medium Effort   ☐ Easy Effort

Average HR: _____ bpm   Target HR: _____ bpm

Feeling: ☐ Fantastic   ☐ Good   ☐ Difficult   ☐ Very Difficult

Weather:

Temperature: _____ ° ___   Workout Gear: _____

Notes: _____

_____

_____

Monday

Vitals:

Resting HR: _____ bpm   Weight: _____ kg/lbs   Hours Slept: _____ hrs

Sport: _____   **Workout:** _____

Course: _____   Duration: _____   Distance: _____

Intensity: ☐ Max. Effort   ☐ Hard Effort   ☐ Medium Effort   ☐ Easy Effort

Average HR: _____ bpm   Target HR: _____ bpm

Feeling: ☐ Fantastic   ☐ Good   ☐ Difficult   ☐ Very Difficult

Weather:

Temperature: _____ ° ___   Workout Gear: _____

Notes: _____

_____

_____

Tuesday

Vitals:

Resting HR: _____ bpm   Weight: _____ kg/lbs   Hours Slept: _____ hrs

Sport: _____   **Workout:** _____

Course: _____   Duration: _____   Distance: _____

Intensity: ☐ Max. Effort   ☐ Hard Effort   ☐ Medium Effort   ☐ Easy Effort

Average HR: _____ bpm   Target HR: _____ bpm

Feeling: ☐ Fantastic   ☐ Good   ☐ Difficult   ☐ Very Difficult

Weather:

Temperature: _____ ° ___   Workout Gear: _____

Notes: _____

_____

_____

Wednesday

Vitals:

Resting HR: _____ bpm   Weight: _____ kg/lbs   Hours Slept: _____ hrs

Sport: _____ **Workout:** _____

Course: _____   Duration: _____   Distance: _____

Intensity: ☐ Max. Effort   ☐ Hard Effort   ☐ Medium Effort   ☐ Easy Effort

Average HR: _____ bpm   Target HR: _____ bpm

Feeling: ☐ Fantastic   ☐ Good   ☐ Difficult   ☐ Very Difficult

Weather:

Temperature: _____ ° ___   Workout Gear: _____

Notes: _____
_____
_____

Thursday

Vitals:

Resting HR: _____ bpm   Weight: _____ kg/lbs   Hours Slept: _____ hrs

Sport: _____ **Workout:** _____

Course: _____   Duration: _____   Distance: _____

Intensity: ☐ Max. Effort   ☐ Hard Effort   ☐ Medium Effort   ☐ Easy Effort

Average HR: _____ bpm   Target HR: _____ bpm

Feeling: ☐ Fantastic   ☐ Good   ☐ Difficult   ☐ Very Difficult

Weather:

Temperature: _____ ° ___   Workout Gear: _____

Notes: _____
_____
_____

Friday

Vitals:

Resting HR: _____ bpm   Weight: _____ kg/lbs   Hours Slept: _____ hrs

Sport: _____ **Workout:** _____

Course: _____   Duration: _____   Distance: _____

Intensity: ☐ Max. Effort   ☐ Hard Effort   ☐ Medium Effort   ☐ Easy Effort

Average HR: _____ bpm   Target HR: _____ bpm

Feeling: ☐ Fantastic   ☐ Good   ☐ Difficult   ☐ Very Difficult

Weather:

Temperature: _____ ° ___   Workout Gear: _____

Notes: _____
_____
_____

Vitals:
Resting HR: _____ bpm   Weight: _____ kg/lbs   Hours Slept: _____ hrs

Sport: _____   Workout: _____

Course: _____   Duration: _____   Distance: _____

Intensity: ☐ Max. Effort   ☐ Hard Effort   ☐ Medium Effort   ☐ Easy Effort

Average HR: _____ bpm   Target HR: _____ bpm

Feeling: ☐ Fantastic   ☐ Good   ☐ Difficult   ☐ Very Difficult

Weather:
Temperature: _____ °____   Workout Gear: _____

Notes: _____
_____

Week Summary

Distance / Time

Sunday   Monday   Tuesday   Wednesday   Thursday   Friday   Saturday

Day

Total Time: _____ Total Distance: _____

Additional Notes: _____
_____
_____
_____
_____
_____

"Do you really
want to get to your
goal? Well,
there's a process. It
involves one step
at a time and it
involves patience."
—Laurie
Skreslet,
first Canadian to
climb Mount
Everest

Vitals:

Resting HR: _____ bpm   Weight: _____ kg/lbs   Hours Slept: _____ hrs

Sport: _____   **Workout:** _____

Course: _____   Duration: _____   Distance: _____

Intensity: ☐ Max. Effort   ☐ Hard Effort   ☐ Medium Effort   ☐ Easy Effort

Average HR: _____ bpm   Target HR: _____ bpm

Feeling: ☐ Fantastic   ☐ Good   ☐ Difficult   ☐ Very Difficult

Weather:

Temperature: _____ ° ___   Workout Gear: _____

Notes: _____

_____

_____

Vitals:

Resting HR: _____ bpm   Weight: _____ kg/lbs   Hours Slept: _____ hrs

Sport: _____   **Workout:** _____

Course: _____   Duration: _____   Distance: _____

Intensity: ☐ Max. Effort   ☐ Hard Effort   ☐ Medium Effort   ☐ Easy Effort

Average HR: _____ bpm   Target HR: _____ bpm

Feeling: ☐ Fantastic   ☐ Good   ☐ Difficult   ☐ Very Difficult

Weather:

Temperature: _____ ° ___   Workout Gear: _____

Notes: _____

_____

_____

Vitals:

Resting HR: _____ bpm   Weight: _____ kg/lbs   Hours Slept: _____ hrs

Sport: _____   **Workout:** _____

Course: _____   Duration: _____   Distance: _____

Intensity: ☐ Max. Effort   ☐ Hard Effort   ☐ Medium Effort   ☐ Easy Effort

Average HR: _____ bpm   Target HR: _____ bpm

Feeling: ☐ Fantastic   ☐ Good   ☐ Difficult   ☐ Very Difficult

Weather:

Temperature: _____ ° ___   Workout Gear: _____

Notes: _____

_____

_____

Vitals:

Resting HR: _____ bpm   Weight: _____ kg/lbs   Hours Slept: _____ hrs

Sport: _____   **Workout:** _____

Course: _____   Duration: _____   Distance: _____

Intensity: ☐ Max. Effort   ☐ Hard Effort   ☐ Medium Effort   ☐ Easy Effort

Average HR: _____ bpm   Target HR: _____ bpm

Feeling: ☐ Fantastic   ☐ Good   ☐ Difficult   ☐ Very Difficult

Weather:

Temperature: _____ ° ___   Workout Gear: _____

Notes: _____

_____

_____

Thursday

Vitals:

Resting HR: _____ bpm   Weight: _____ kg/lbs   Hours Slept: _____ hrs

Sport: _____   **Workout:** _____

Course: _____   Duration: _____   Distance: _____

Intensity: ☐ Max. Effort   ☐ Hard Effort   ☐ Medium Effort   ☐ Easy Effort

Average HR: _____ bpm   Target HR: _____ bpm

Feeling: ☐ Fantastic   ☐ Good   ☐ Difficult   ☐ Very Difficult

Weather:

Temperature: _____ ° ___   Workout Gear: _____

Notes: _____

_____

_____

Friday

Vitals:

Resting HR: _____ bpm   Weight: _____ kg/lbs   Hours Slept: _____ hrs

Sport: _____   **Workout:** _____

Course: _____   Duration: _____   Distance: _____

Intensity: ☐ Max. Effort   ☐ Hard Effort   ☐ Medium Effort   ☐ Easy Effort

Average HR: _____ bpm   Target HR: _____ bpm

Feeling: ☐ Fantastic   ☐ Good   ☐ Difficult   ☐ Very Difficult

Weather:

Temperature: _____ ° ___   Workout Gear: _____

Notes: _____

_____

_____

Vitals:

Resting HR: _____ bpm   Weight: _____ kg/lbs   Hours Slept: _____ hrs

Sport: _____   **Workout:** _____

Course: _____   Duration: _____   Distance: _____

Intensity: ☐ Max. Effort   ☐ Hard Effort   ☐ Medium Effort   ☐ Easy Effort

Average HR: _____ bpm   Target HR: _____ bpm

Feeling: ☐ Fantastic   ☐ Good   ☐ Difficult   ☐ Very Difficult

Weather:

Temperature: _____ ° ___   Workout Gear: _____

Notes: _____

_____

_____

Week Summary

Distance / Time

Sunday   Monday   Tuesday   Wednesday   Thursday   Friday   Saturday

Day

Total Time: _____ Total Distance: _____

Additional Notes: _____

_____

_____

_____

_____

_____

"It is only the farmer who
faithfully plants seeds in the
spring who reaps a Harvest
in the autumn." — B.C. Forbes

Vitals:

Resting HR: _____ bpm   Weight: _____ kg/lbs   Hours Slept: _____ hrs

Sport: _____   **Workout:** _____

Course: _____   Duration: _____   Distance: _____

Intensity: ☐ Max. Effort   ☐ Hard Effort   ☐ Medium Effort   ☐ Easy Effort

Average HR: _____ bpm   Target HR: _____ bpm

Feeling: ☐ Fantastic   ☐ Good   ☐ Difficult   ☐ Very Difficult

Weather:

Temperature: _____°___   Workout Gear: _____

Notes: _____

_____

_____

Monday

Vitals:

Resting HR: _____ bpm   Weight: _____ kg/lbs   Hours Slept: _____ hrs

Sport: _____   **Workout:** _____

Course: _____   Duration: _____   Distance: _____

Intensity: ☐ Max. Effort   ☐ Hard Effort   ☐ Medium Effort   ☐ Easy Effort

Average HR: _____ bpm   Target HR: _____ bpm

Feeling: ☐ Fantastic   ☐ Good   ☐ Difficult   ☐ Very Difficult

Weather:

Temperature: _____°___   Workout Gear: _____

Notes: _____

_____

_____

Tuesday

Vitals:

Resting HR: _____ bpm   Weight: _____ kg/lbs   Hours Slept: _____ hrs

Sport: _____   **Workout:** _____

Course: _____   Duration: _____   Distance: _____

Intensity: ☐ Max. Effort   ☐ Hard Effort   ☐ Medium Effort   ☐ Easy Effort

Average HR: _____ bpm   Target HR: _____ bpm

Feeling: ☐ Fantastic   ☐ Good   ☐ Difficult   ☐ Very Difficult

Weather:

Temperature: _____°___   Workout Gear: _____

Notes: _____

_____

_____

Vitals:

Resting HR: _____ bpm   Weight: _____ kg/lbs   Hours Slept: _____ hrs

Sport: _____ **Workout:** _____

Course: _____   Duration: _____   Distance: _____

Intensity: ☐ Max. Effort   ☐ Hard Effort   ☐ Medium Effort   ☐ Easy Effort

Average HR: _____ bpm   Target HR: _____ bpm

Feeling: ☐ Fantastic   ☐ Good   ☐ Difficult   ☐ Very Difficult

Weather:

Temperature: _____ ° ___   Workout Gear: _____

Notes: _____

_____

_____

Thursday

Vitals:

Resting HR: _____ bpm   Weight: _____ kg/lbs   Hours Slept: _____ hrs

Sport: _____ **Workout:** _____

Course: _____   Duration: _____   Distance: _____

Intensity: ☐ Max. Effort   ☐ Hard Effort   ☐ Medium Effort   ☐ Easy Effort

Average HR: _____ bpm   Target HR: _____ bpm

Feeling: ☐ Fantastic   ☐ Good   ☐ Difficult   ☐ Very Difficult

Weather:

Temperature: _____ ° ___   Workout Gear: _____

Notes: _____

_____

_____

Friday

Vitals:

Resting HR: _____ bpm   Weight: _____ kg/lbs   Hours Slept: _____ hrs

Sport: _____ **Workout:** _____

Course: _____   Duration: _____   Distance: _____

Intensity: ☐ Max. Effort   ☐ Hard Effort   ☐ Medium Effort   ☐ Easy Effort

Average HR: _____ bpm   Target HR: _____ bpm

Feeling: ☐ Fantastic   ☐ Good   ☐ Difficult   ☐ Very Difficult

Weather:

Temperature: _____ ° ___   Workout Gear: _____

Notes: _____

_____

_____

Week 37   Date: ☐ ☐ ☐   Saturday

Vitals:

Resting HR: _____ bpm   Weight: _____ kg/lbs   Hours Slept: _____ hrs

Sport: _____   **Workout:** _____

Course: _____   Duration: _____   Distance: _____

Intensity: ☐ Max. Effort   ☐ Hard Effort   ☐ Medium Effort   ☐ Easy Effort

Average HR: _____ bpm   Target HR: _____ bpm

Feeling: ☐ Fantastic   ☐ Good   ☐ Difficult   ☐ Very Difficult

Weather:

Temperature: _____ ° ___   Workout Gear: _____

Notes: _____

_____

Week Summary

Total Time: _____ Total Distance: _____

Additional Notes: _____

_____
_____
_____
_____

"Life is
short...
running
makes
it seem
longer."

— Baron Hansen

Vitals:

Resting HR: _____ bpm   Weight: _____ kg/lbs   Hours Slept: _____ hrs

Sport: _____   Workout: _____

Course: _____   Duration: _____   Distance: _____

Intensity: ☐ Max. Effort   ☐ Hard Effort   ☐ Medium Effort   ☐ Easy Effort

Average HR: _____ bpm   Target HR: _____ bpm

Feeling: ☐ Fantastic   ☐ Good   ☐ Difficult   ☐ Very Difficult

Weather:

Temperature: _____ ° ___   Workout Gear: _____

Notes: _____

_____

_____

Monday

Vitals:

Resting HR: _____ bpm   Weight: _____ kg/lbs   Hours Slept: _____ hrs

Sport: _____   Workout: _____

Course: _____   Duration: _____   Distance: _____

Intensity: ☐ Max. Effort   ☐ Hard Effort   ☐ Medium Effort   ☐ Easy Effort

Average HR: _____ bpm   Target HR: _____ bpm

Feeling: ☐ Fantastic   ☐ Good   ☐ Difficult   ☐ Very Difficult

Weather:

Temperature: _____ ° ___   Workout Gear: _____

Notes: _____

_____

_____

Tuesday

Vitals:

Resting HR: _____ bpm   Weight: _____ kg/lbs   Hours Slept: _____ hrs

Sport: _____   Workout: _____

Course: _____   Duration: _____   Distance: _____

Intensity: ☐ Max. Effort   ☐ Hard Effort   ☐ Medium Effort   ☐ Easy Effort

Average HR: _____ bpm   Target HR: _____ bpm

Feeling: ☐ Fantastic   ☐ Good   ☐ Difficult   ☐ Very Difficult

Weather:

Temperature: _____ ° ___   Workout Gear: _____

Notes: _____

_____

_____

Vitals:

Resting HR: _____ bpm   Weight: _____ kg/lbs   Hours Slept: _____ hrs

Sport: _____   **Workout:** _____

Course: _____   Duration: _____   Distance: _____

Intensity: ☐ Max. Effort   ☐ Hard Effort   ☐ Medium Effort   ☐ Easy Effort

Average HR: _____ bpm   Target HR: _____ bpm

Feeling: ☐ Fantastic   ☐ Good   ☐ Difficult   ☐ Very Difficult

Weather:

Temperature: _____ ° ___   Workout Gear: _____

Notes: _____

_____

_____

Thursday

Vitals:

Resting HR: _____ bpm   Weight: _____ kg/lbs   Hours Slept: _____ hrs

Sport: _____   **Workout:** _____

Course: _____   Duration: _____   Distance: _____

Intensity: ☐ Max. Effort   ☐ Hard Effort   ☐ Medium Effort   ☐ Easy Effort

Average HR: _____ bpm   Target HR: _____ bpm

Feeling: ☐ Fantastic   ☐ Good   ☐ Difficult   ☐ Very Difficult

Weather:

Temperature: _____ ° ___   Workout Gear: _____

Notes: _____

_____

_____

Friday

Vitals:

Resting HR: _____ bpm   Weight: _____ kg/lbs   Hours Slept: _____ hrs

Sport: _____   **Workout:** _____

Course: _____   Duration: _____   Distance: _____

Intensity: ☐ Max. Effort   ☐ Hard Effort   ☐ Medium Effort   ☐ Easy Effort

Average HR: _____ bpm   Target HR: _____ bpm

Feeling: ☐ Fantastic   ☐ Good   ☐ Difficult   ☐ Very Difficult

Weather:

Temperature: _____ ° ___   Workout Gear: _____

Notes: _____

_____

_____

Vitals:

Resting HR: _____ bpm   Weight: _____ kg/lbs   Hours Slept: _____ hrs

Sport: _____ Workout: _____

Course: _____   Duration: _____   Distance: _____

Intensity: ☐ Max. Effort   ☐ Hard Effort   ☐ Medium Effort   ☐ Easy Effort

Average HR: _____ bpm   Target HR: _____ bpm

Feeling: ☐ Fantastic   ☐ Good   ☐ Difficult   ☐ Very Difficult

Weather:

Temperature: _____ ° ___   Workout Gear: _____

Notes: _____

_____

_____

Week Summary

Distance / Time

| | Sunday | Monday | Tuesday | Wednesday | Thursday | Friday | Saturday |

Day

Total Time: _____ Total Distance: _____

Additional Notes: _____ _____

_____

_____

_____

_____

_____

"THE GUN GOES OFF AND EVERTHING
CHANGES... THE WORLD CHANGES...
AND NOTHING ELSE REALLY MATTERS."
— PATTI SUE PLUMMER

Vitals:

Resting HR: _____ bpm   Weight: _____ kg/lbs   Hours Slept: _____ hrs

Sport: _____   **Workout:** _____

Course: _____   Duration: _____   Distance: _____

Intensity: ☐ Max. Effort ☐ Hard Effort ☐ Medium Effort ☐ Easy Effort

Average HR: _____ bpm   Target HR: _____ bpm

Feeling: ☐ Fantastic ☐ Good ☐ Difficult ☐ Very Difficult

Weather:

Temperature: _____ ° ___   Workout Gear: _____

Notes: _____

_____

_____

Monday

Vitals:

Resting HR: _____ bpm   Weight: _____ kg/lbs   Hours Slept: _____ hrs

Sport: _____   **Workout:** _____

Course: _____   Duration: _____   Distance: _____

Intensity: ☐ Max. Effort ☐ Hard Effort ☐ Medium Effort ☐ Easy Effort

Average HR: _____ bpm   Target HR: _____ bpm

Feeling: ☐ Fantastic ☐ Good ☐ Difficult ☐ Very Difficult

Weather:

Temperature: _____ ° ___   Workout Gear: _____

Notes: _____

_____

_____

Tuesday

Vitals:

Resting HR: _____ bpm   Weight: _____ kg/lbs   Hours Slept: _____ hrs

Sport: _____   **Workout:** _____

Course: _____   Duration: _____   Distance: _____

Intensity: ☐ Max. Effort ☐ Hard Effort ☐ Medium Effort ☐ Easy Effort

Average HR: _____ bpm   Target HR: _____ bpm

Feeling: ☐ Fantastic ☐ Good ☐ Difficult ☐ Very Difficult

Weather:

Temperature: _____ ° ___   Workout Gear: _____

Notes: _____

_____

_____

Vitals:

Resting HR: _____ bpm   Weight: _____ kg/lbs   Hours Slept: _____ hrs

Sport: _____   **Workout:** _____

Course: _____   Duration: _____   Distance: _____

Intensity: ☐ Max. Effort   ☐ Hard Effort   ☐ Medium Effort   ☐ Easy Effort

Average HR: _____ bpm   Target HR: _____ bpm

Feeling: ☐ Fantastic   ☐ Good   ☐ Difficult   ☐ Very Difficult

Weather:

Temperature: _____ ° ___   Workout Gear: _____

Notes: _____

_____

_____

Thursday

Vitals:

Resting HR: _____ bpm   Weight: _____ kg/lbs   Hours Slept: _____ hrs

Sport: _____   **Workout:** _____

Course: _____   Duration: _____   Distance: _____

Intensity: ☐ Max. Effort   ☐ Hard Effort   ☐ Medium Effort   ☐ Easy Effort

Average HR: _____ bpm   Target HR: _____ bpm

Feeling: ☐ Fantastic   ☐ Good   ☐ Difficult   ☐ Very Difficult

Weather:

Temperature: _____ ° ___   Workout Gear: _____

Notes: _____

_____

_____

Friday

Vitals:

Resting HR: _____ bpm   Weight: _____ kg/lbs   Hours Slept: _____ hrs

Sport: _____   **Workout:** _____

Course: _____   Duration: _____   Distance: _____

Intensity: ☐ Max. Effort   ☐ Hard Effort   ☐ Medium Effort   ☐ Easy Effort

Average HR: _____ bpm   Target HR: _____ bpm

Feeling: ☐ Fantastic   ☐ Good   ☐ Difficult   ☐ Very Difficult

Weather:

Temperature: _____ ° ___   Workout Gear: _____

Notes: _____

_____

_____

Vitals:

Resting HR: _____ bpm　　Weight: _____ kg/lbs　Hours Slept: _____ hrs

Sport: _____　Workout: _____

Course: _____　Duration: _____　Distance: _____

Intensity:　☐ Max. Effort　☐ Hard Effort　☐ Medium Effort　☐ Easy Effort

Average HR: _____ bpm　　Target HR: _____ bpm

Feeling:　☐ Fantastic　☐ Good　☐ Difficult　☐ Very Difficult

Weather:

Temperature: _____ ° ___　Workout Gear: _____

Notes: _____

_____

_____

Week Summary

Distance / Time

	Sunday	Monday	Tuesday	Wednesday	Thursday	Friday	Saturday

Day

Total Time: _____ Total Distance: _____

Additional Notes: _____

_____

_____

_____

_____

Vitals:

Resting HR: _____ bpm   Weight: _____ kg/lbs   Hours Slept: _____ hrs

Sport: _____   **Workout:** _____

Course: _____   Duration: _____   Distance: _____

Intensity: ☐ Max. Effort   ☐ Hard Effort   ☐ Medium Effort   ☐ Easy Effort

Average HR: _____ bpm   Target HR: _____ bpm

Feeling: ☐ Fantastic   ☐ Good   ☐ Difficult   ☐ Very Difficult

Weather:

Temperature: _____ ° ___   Workout Gear: _____

Notes: _____
_____
_____

Monday

Vitals:

Resting HR: _____ bpm   Weight: _____ kg/lbs   Hours Slept: _____ hrs

Sport: _____   **Workout:** _____

Course: _____   Duration: _____   Distance: _____

Intensity: ☐ Max. Effort   ☐ Hard Effort   ☐ Medium Effort   ☐ Easy Effort

Average HR: _____ bpm   Target HR: _____ bpm

Feeling: ☐ Fantastic   ☐ Good   ☐ Difficult   ☐ Very Difficult

Weather:

Temperature: _____ ° ___   Workout Gear: _____

Notes: _____
_____
_____

Tuesday

Vitals:

Resting HR: _____ bpm   Weight: _____ kg/lbs   Hours Slept: _____ hrs

Sport: _____   **Workout:** _____

Course: _____   Duration: _____   Distance: _____

Intensity: ☐ Max. Effort   ☐ Hard Effort   ☐ Medium Effort   ☐ Easy Effort

Average HR: _____ bpm   Target HR: _____ bpm

Feeling: ☐ Fantastic   ☐ Good   ☐ Difficult   ☐ Very Difficult

Weather:

Temperature: _____ ° ___   Workout Gear: _____

Notes: _____
_____
_____

Vitals:

Resting HR: _____ bpm   Weight: _____ kg/lbs   Hours Slept: _____ hrs

Sport: _____   **Workout:** _____

Course: _____   Duration: _____   Distance: _____

Intensity: ☐ Max. Effort   ☐ Hard Effort   ☐ Medium Effort   ☐ Easy Effort

Average HR: _____ bpm   Target HR: _____ bpm

Feeling: ☐ Fantastic   ☐ Good   ☐ Difficult   ☐ Very Difficult

Weather:

Temperature: _____ ° ___   Workout Gear: _____

Notes: _____
_____
_____

Thursday

Vitals:

Resting HR: _____ bpm   Weight: _____ kg/lbs   Hours Slept: _____ hrs

Sport: _____   **Workout:** _____

Course: _____   Duration: _____   Distance: _____

Intensity: ☐ Max. Effort   ☐ Hard Effort   ☐ Medium Effort   ☐ Easy Effort

Average HR: _____ bpm   Target HR: _____ bpm

Feeling: ☐ Fantastic   ☐ Good   ☐ Difficult   ☐ Very Difficult

Weather:

Temperature: _____ ° ___   Workout Gear: _____

Notes: _____
_____
_____

Friday

Vitals:

Resting HR: _____ bpm   Weight: _____ kg/lbs   Hours Slept: _____ hrs

Sport: _____   **Workout:** _____

Course: _____   Duration: _____   Distance: _____

Intensity: ☐ Max. Effort   ☐ Hard Effort   ☐ Medium Effort   ☐ Easy Effort

Average HR: _____ bpm   Target HR: _____ bpm

Feeling: ☐ Fantastic   ☐ Good   ☐ Difficult   ☐ Very Difficult

Weather:

Temperature: _____ ° ___   Workout Gear: _____

Notes: _____
_____
_____

Vitals:

Resting HR: _____ bpm   Weight: _____ kg/lbs   Hours Slept: _____ hrs

Sport: _____   Workout: _____

Course: _____   Duration: _____   Distance: _____

Intensity: ☐ Max. Effort   ☐ Hard Effort   ☐ Medium Effort   ☐ Easy Effort

Average HR: _____ bpm   Target HR: _____ bpm

Feeling: ☐ Fantastic   ☐ Good   ☐ Difficult   ☐ Very Difficult

Weather:

Temperature: _____ ° ___   Workout Gear: _____

Notes: _____
_____
_____

Week Summary

Distance / Time

Sunday   Monday   Tuesday   Wednesday   Thursday   Friday   Saturday

Day

Total Time: _____ Total Distance: _____

Additional Notes: _____
_____
_____
_____
_____
_____

"SOMEWHERE IN THE WORLD SOMEONE IS TRAINING WHEN YOU ARE NOT. WHEN YOU RACE HIM, HE WILL WIN." —TOM FLEMING'S BOSTON MARATHON TRAINING SIGN ON HIS WALL

Mizuno

IAAF IAAF IAAF IAAF IAAF

Vitals:

Resting HR: _____ bpm   Weight: _____ kg/lbs   Hours Slept: _____ hrs

Sport: _____   **Workout:** _____

Course: _____   Duration: _____   Distance: _____

Intensity: ☐ Max. Effort   ☐ Hard Effort   ☐ Medium Effort   ☐ Easy Effort

Average HR: _____ bpm   Target HR: _____ bpm

Feeling: ☐ Fantastic   ☐ Good   ☐ Difficult   ☐ Very Difficult

Weather:

Temperature: _____ ° ___   Workout Gear: _____

Notes: _____

_____

_____

Monday

Vitals:

Resting HR: _____ bpm   Weight: _____ kg/lbs   Hours Slept: _____ hrs

Sport: _____   **Workout:** _____

Course: _____   Duration: _____   Distance: _____

Intensity: ☐ Max. Effort   ☐ Hard Effort   ☐ Medium Effort   ☐ Easy Effort

Average HR: _____ bpm   Target HR: _____ bpm

Feeling: ☐ Fantastic   ☐ Good   ☐ Difficult   ☐ Very Difficult

Weather:

Temperature: _____ ° ___   Workout Gear: _____

Notes: _____

_____

_____

Tuesday

Vitals:

Resting HR: _____ bpm   Weight: _____ kg/lbs   Hours Slept: _____ hrs

Sport: _____   **Workout:** _____

Course: _____   Duration: _____   Distance: _____

Intensity: ☐ Max. Effort   ☐ Hard Effort   ☐ Medium Effort   ☐ Easy Effort

Average HR: _____ bpm   Target HR: _____ bpm

Feeling: ☐ Fantastic   ☐ Good   ☐ Difficult   ☐ Very Difficult

Weather:

Temperature: _____ ° ___   Workout Gear: _____

Notes: _____

_____

_____

Wednesday Week 41

Vitals:

Resting HR: _____ bpm   Weight: _____ kg/lbs   Hours Slept: _____ hrs

Sport: _____   **Workout:** _____

Course: _____   Duration: _____   Distance: _____

Intensity: ☐ Max. Effort   ☐ Hard Effort   ☐ Medium Effort   ☐ Easy Effort

Average HR: _____ bpm   Target HR: _____ bpm

Feeling: ☐ Fantastic   ☐ Good   ☐ Difficult   ☐ Very Difficult

Weather:

Temperature: _____°___   Workout Gear: _____

Notes: _____
_____
_____

Thursday

Vitals:

Resting HR: _____ bpm   Weight: _____ kg/lbs   Hours Slept: _____ hrs

Sport: _____   **Workout:** _____

Course: _____   Duration: _____   Distance: _____

Intensity: ☐ Max. Effort   ☐ Hard Effort   ☐ Medium Effort   ☐ Easy Effort

Average HR: _____ bpm   Target HR: _____ bpm

Feeling: ☐ Fantastic   ☐ Good   ☐ Difficult   ☐ Very Difficult

Weather:

Temperature: _____°___   Workout Gear: _____

Notes: _____
_____
_____

Friday

Vitals:

Resting HR: _____ bpm   Weight: _____ kg/lbs   Hours Slept: _____ hrs

Sport: _____   **Workout:** _____

Course: _____   Duration: _____   Distance: _____

Intensity: ☐ Max. Effort   ☐ Hard Effort   ☐ Medium Effort   ☐ Easy Effort

Average HR: _____ bpm   Target HR: _____ bpm

Feeling: ☐ Fantastic   ☐ Good   ☐ Difficult   ☐ Very Difficult

Weather:

Temperature: _____°___   Workout Gear: _____

Notes: _____
_____
_____

Vitals:

Resting HR: _____ bpm   Weight: _____ kg/lbs   Hours Slept: _____ hrs

Sport: _____   Workout: _____

Course: _____   Duration: _____   Distance: _____

Intensity: ▢ Max. Effort   ▢ Hard Effort   ▢ Medium Effort   ▢ Easy Effort

Average HR: _____ bpm   Target HR: _____ bpm

Feeling: ▢ Fantastic   ▢ Good   ▢ Difficult   ▢ Very Difficult

Weather:

Temperature: _____ ° ___   Workout Gear: _____

Notes: _____

_____

_____

Week Summary

Distance / Time

Sunday   Monday   Tuesday   Wednesday   Thursday   Friday   Saturday

Day

Total Time: _____ Total Distance: _____

Additional Notes: _____

_____

_____

_____

_____

_____

"We should not let our fears hold us back from pursuing our hopes."
— John F. Kennedy

Vitals:
Resting HR: _____ bpm   Weight: _____ kg/lbs   Hours Slept: _____ hrs

Sport: _____   **Workout:** _____

Course: _____   Duration: _____   Distance: _____

Intensity: ☐ Max. Effort   ☐ Hard Effort   ☐ Medium Effort   ☐ Easy Effort

Average HR: _____ bpm   Target HR: _____ bpm

Feeling: ☐ Fantastic   ☐ Good   ☐ Difficult   ☐ Very Difficult

Weather:
Temperature: _____ ° ___   Workout Gear: _____

Notes: _____
_____
_____

Vitals:
Resting HR: _____ bpm   Weight: _____ kg/lbs   Hours Slept: _____ hrs

Sport: _____   **Workout:** _____

Course: _____   Duration: _____   Distance: _____

Intensity: ☐ Max. Effort   ☐ Hard Effort   ☐ Medium Effort   ☐ Easy Effort

Average HR: _____ bpm   Target HR: _____ bpm

Feeling: ☐ Fantastic   ☐ Good   ☐ Difficult   ☐ Very Difficult

Weather:
Temperature: _____ ° ___   Workout Gear: _____

Notes: _____
_____
_____

Vitals:
Resting HR: _____ bpm   Weight: _____ kg/lbs   Hours Slept: _____ hrs

Sport: _____   **Workout:** _____

Course: _____   Duration: _____   Distance: _____

Intensity: ☐ Max. Effort   ☐ Hard Effort   ☐ Medium Effort   ☐ Easy Effort

Average HR: _____ bpm   Target HR: _____ bpm

Feeling: ☐ Fantastic   ☐ Good   ☐ Difficult   ☐ Very Difficult

Weather:
Temperature: _____ ° ___   Workout Gear: _____

Notes: _____
_____
_____

Wednesday Week 42

Vitals:

Resting HR: _____ bpm   Weight: _____ kg/lbs   Hours Slept: _____ hrs

Sport: _____   **Workout:** _____

Course: _____   Duration: _____   Distance: _____

Intensity: ☐ Max. Effort   ☐ Hard Effort   ☐ Medium Effort   ☐ Easy Effort

Average HR: _____ bpm   Target HR: _____ bpm

Feeling: ☐ Fantastic   ☐ Good   ☐ Difficult   ☐ Very Difficult

Weather:

Temperature: _____ ° ___   Workout Gear: _____

Notes: _____
_____
_____

Thursday

Vitals:

Resting HR: _____ bpm   Weight: _____ kg/lbs   Hours Slept: _____ hrs

Sport: _____   **Workout:** _____

Course: _____   Duration: _____   Distance: _____

Intensity: ☐ Max. Effort   ☐ Hard Effort   ☐ Medium Effort   ☐ Easy Effort

Average HR: _____ bpm   Target HR: _____ bpm

Feeling: ☐ Fantastic   ☐ Good   ☐ Difficult   ☐ Very Difficult

Weather:

Temperature: _____ ° ___   Workout Gear: _____

Notes: _____
_____
_____

Friday

Vitals:

Resting HR: _____ bpm   Weight: _____ kg/lbs   Hours Slept: _____ hrs

Sport: _____   **Workout:** _____

Course: _____   Duration: _____   Distance: _____

Intensity: ☐ Max. Effort   ☐ Hard Effort   ☐ Medium Effort   ☐ Easy Effort

Average HR: _____ bpm   Target HR: _____ bpm

Feeling: ☐ Fantastic   ☐ Good   ☐ Difficult   ☐ Very Difficult

Weather:

Temperature: _____ ° ___   Workout Gear: _____

Notes: _____
_____
_____

Vitals:
Resting HR: _____ bpm   Weight: _____ kg/lbs   Hours Slept: _____ hrs

Sport: _____ Workout: _____

Course: _____   Duration: _____   Distance: _____

Intensity: ☐ Max. Effort   ☐ Hard Effort   ☐ Medium Effort   ☐ Easy Effort

Average HR: _____ bpm   Target HR: _____ bpm

Feeling: ☐ Fantastic   ☐ Good   ☐ Difficult   ☐ Very Difficult

Weather:
Temperature: _____ ° ___   Workout Gear: _____

Notes: _____
_____
_____

Week Summary

Distance / Time vs Day

Sunday Monday Tuesday Wednesday Thursday Friday Saturday

Day

Total Time: _____ Total Distance: _____

Additional Notes: _____
_____
_____
_____
_____
_____

"All that running
and exercise can
do for you is make
you healthy."
— Denny McLain

Vitals:

Resting HR: _____ bpm   Weight: _____ kg/lbs   Hours Slept: _____ hrs

Sport: _____   **Workout:** _____

Course: _____   Duration: _____   Distance: _____

Intensity: ☐ Max. Effort   ☐ Hard Effort   ☐ Medium Effort   ☐ Easy Effort

Average HR: _____ bpm   Target HR: _____ bpm

Feeling: ☐ Fantastic   ☐ Good   ☐ Difficult   ☐ Very Difficult

Weather:

Temperature: _____ ° ___   Workout Gear: _____

Notes: _____
_____
_____

Monday

Vitals:

Resting HR: _____ bpm   Weight: _____ kg/lbs   Hours Slept: _____ hrs

Sport: _____   **Workout:** _____

Course: _____   Duration: _____   Distance: _____

Intensity: ☐ Max. Effort   ☐ Hard Effort   ☐ Medium Effort   ☐ Easy Effort

Average HR: _____ bpm   Target HR: _____ bpm

Feeling: ☐ Fantastic   ☐ Good   ☐ Difficult   ☐ Very Difficult

Weather:

Temperature: _____ ° ___   Workout Gear: _____

Notes: _____
_____
_____

Tuesday

Vitals:

Resting HR: _____ bpm   Weight: _____ kg/lbs   Hours Slept: _____ hrs

Sport: _____   **Workout:** _____

Course: _____   Duration: _____   Distance: _____

Intensity: ☐ Max. Effort   ☐ Hard Effort   ☐ Medium Effort   ☐ Easy Effort

Average HR: _____ bpm   Target HR: _____ bpm

Feeling: ☐ Fantastic   ☐ Good   ☐ Difficult   ☐ Very Difficult

Weather:

Temperature: _____ ° ___   Workout Gear: _____

Notes: _____
_____
_____

Vitals:

Resting HR: _____ bpm   Weight: _____ kg/lbs   Hours Slept: _____ hrs

Sport: _____ **Workout:** _____

Course: _____   Duration: _____   Distance: _____

Intensity: □ Max. Effort   □ Hard Effort   □ Medium Effort   □ Easy Effort

Average HR: _____ bpm   Target HR: _____ bpm

Feeling: □ Fantastic   □ Good   □ Difficult   □ Very Difficult

Weather:

Temperature: _____ ° ___   Workout Gear: _____

Notes: _____

_____

_____

Vitals:

Resting HR: _____ bpm   Weight: _____ kg/lbs   Hours Slept: _____ hrs

Sport: _____ **Workout:** _____

Course: _____   Duration: _____   Distance: _____

Intensity: □ Max. Effort   □ Hard Effort   □ Medium Effort   □ Easy Effort

Average HR: _____ bpm   Target HR: _____ bpm

Feeling: □ Fantastic   □ Good   □ Difficult   □ Very Difficult

Weather:

Temperature: _____ ° ___   Workout Gear: _____

Notes: _____

_____

_____

Vitals:

Resting HR: _____ bpm   Weight: _____ kg/lbs   Hours Slept: _____ hrs

Sport: _____ **Workout:** _____

Course: _____   Duration: _____   Distance: _____

Intensity: □ Max. Effort   □ Hard Effort   □ Medium Effort   □ Easy Effort

Average HR: _____ bpm   Target HR: _____ bpm

Feeling: □ Fantastic   □ Good   □ Difficult   □ Very Difficult

Weather:

Temperature: _____ ° ___   Workout Gear: _____

Notes: _____

_____

_____

Week 43   Date: ▮ ▮ ▮   Saturday

Vitals:
Resting HR: _____ bpm   Weight: _____ kg/lbs   Hours Slept: _____ hrs

Sport: _____   Workout: _____

Course: _____   Duration: _____   Distance: _____

Intensity: ☐ Max. Effort ☐ Hard Effort ☐ Medium Effort ☐ Easy Effort

Average HR: _____ bpm   Target HR: _____ bpm

Feeling: ☐ Fantastic ☐ Good ☐ Difficult ☐ Very Difficult

Weather:
Temperature: _____ ° _____   Workout Gear: _____

Notes: _____
_____
_____

Week Summary

Total Time: _____ Total Distance: _____

Additional Notes: _____
_____
_____
_____
_____

230

Vitals:

Resting HR: _____ bpm   Weight: _____ kg/lbs   Hours Slept: _____ hrs

Sport: _____   **Workout:** _____

Course: _____   Duration: _____   Distance: _____

Intensity: ☐ Max. Effort   ☐ Hard Effort   ☐ Medium Effort   ☐ Easy Effort

Average HR: _____ bpm   Target HR: _____ bpm

Feeling: ☐ Fantastic   ☐ Good   ☐ Difficult   ☐ Very Difficult

Weather:

Temperature: _____ ° ___   Workout Gear: _____

Notes: _____

_____

_____

Monday

Vitals:

Resting HR: _____ bpm   Weight: _____ kg/lbs   Hours Slept: _____ hrs

Sport: _____   **Workout:** _____

Course: _____   Duration: _____   Distance: _____

Intensity: ☐ Max. Effort   ☐ Hard Effort   ☐ Medium Effort   ☐ Easy Effort

Average HR: _____ bpm   Target HR: _____ bpm

Feeling: ☐ Fantastic   ☐ Good   ☐ Difficult   ☐ Very Difficult

Weather:

Temperature: _____ ° ___   Workout Gear: _____

Notes: _____

_____

_____

Tuesday

Vitals:

Resting HR: _____ bpm   Weight: _____ kg/lbs   Hours Slept: _____ hrs

Sport: _____   **Workout:** _____

Course: _____   Duration: _____   Distance: _____

Intensity: ☐ Max. Effort   ☐ Hard Effort   ☐ Medium Effort   ☐ Easy Effort

Average HR: _____ bpm   Target HR: _____ bpm

Feeling: ☐ Fantastic   ☐ Good   ☐ Difficult   ☐ Very Difficult

Weather:

Temperature: _____ ° ___   Workout Gear: _____

Notes: _____

_____

_____

Vitals:

Resting HR: _____ bpm   Weight: _____ kg/lbs   Hours Slept: _____ hrs

Sport: _____   **Workout:** _____

Course: _____   Duration: _____   Distance: _____

Intensity: ☐ Max. Effort   ☐ Hard Effort   ☐ Medium Effort   ☐ Easy Effort

Average HR: _____ bpm   Target HR: _____ bpm

Feeling: ☐ Fantastic   ☐ Good   ☐ Difficult   ☐ Very Difficult

Weather:

Temperature: _____ ° ___   Workout Gear: _____

Notes: _____

_____

_____

Thursday

Vitals:

Resting HR: _____ bpm   Weight: _____ kg/lbs   Hours Slept: _____ hrs

Sport: _____   **Workout:** _____

Course: _____   Duration: _____   Distance: _____

Intensity: ☐ Max. Effort   ☐ Hard Effort   ☐ Medium Effort   ☐ Easy Effort

Average HR: _____ bpm   Target HR: _____ bpm

Feeling: ☐ Fantastic   ☐ Good   ☐ Difficult   ☐ Very Difficult

Weather:

Temperature: _____ ° ___   Workout Gear: _____

Notes: _____

_____

_____

Friday

Vitals:

Resting HR: _____ bpm   Weight: _____ kg/lbs   Hours Slept: _____ hrs

Sport: _____   **Workout:** _____

Course: _____   Duration: _____   Distance: _____

Intensity: ☐ Max. Effort   ☐ Hard Effort   ☐ Medium Effort   ☐ Easy Effort

Average HR: _____ bpm   Target HR: _____ bpm

Feeling: ☐ Fantastic   ☐ Good   ☐ Difficult   ☐ Very Difficult

Weather:

Temperature: _____ ° ___   Workout Gear: _____

Notes: _____

_____

_____

Vitals:

Resting HR: _____ bpm   Weight: _____ kg/lbs   Hours Slept: _____ hrs

Sport: _____   Workout: _____

Course: _____   Duration: _____   Distance: _____

Intensity: ☐ Max. Effort   ☐ Hard Effort   ☐ Medium Effort   ☐ Easy Effort

Average HR: _____ bpm   Target HR: _____ bpm

Feeling: ☐ Fantastic   ☐ Good   ☐ Difficult   ☐ Very Difficult

Weather:

Temperature: _____ °___   Workout Gear: _____

Notes: _____
_____
_____

Week Summary

Distance / Time

	Sunday	Monday	Tuesday	Wednesday	Thursday	Friday	Saturday

Day

Total Time: _____ Total Distance: _____

Additional Notes: _____
_____
_____
_____
_____
_____

Vitals:

Resting HR: _____ bpm   Weight: _____ kg/lbs   Hours Slept: _____ hrs

Sport: _____   **Workout:** _____

Course: _____   Duration: _____   Distance: _____

Intensity: ☐ Max. Effort ☐ Hard Effort ☐ Medium Effort ☐ Easy Effort

Average HR: _____ bpm   Target HR: _____ bpm

Feeling: ☐ Fantastic ☐ Good ☐ Difficult ☐ Very Difficult

Weather:

Temperature: _____ ° ___   Workout Gear: _____

Notes: _____

_____

_____

Monday

Vitals:

Resting HR: _____ bpm   Weight: _____ kg/lbs   Hours Slept: _____ hrs

Sport: _____   **Workout:** _____

Course: _____   Duration: _____   Distance: _____

Intensity: ☐ Max. Effort ☐ Hard Effort ☐ Medium Effort ☐ Easy Effort

Average HR: _____ bpm   Target HR: _____ bpm

Feeling: ☐ Fantastic ☐ Good ☐ Difficult ☐ Very Difficult

Weather:

Temperature: _____ ° ___   Workout Gear: _____

Notes: _____

_____

_____

Tuesday

Vitals:

Resting HR: _____ bpm   Weight: _____ kg/lbs   Hours Slept: _____ hrs

Sport: _____   **Workout:** _____

Course: _____   Duration: _____   Distance: _____

Intensity: ☐ Max. Effort ☐ Hard Effort ☐ Medium Effort ☐ Easy Effort

Average HR: _____ bpm   Target HR: _____ bpm

Feeling: ☐ Fantastic ☐ Good ☐ Difficult ☐ Very Difficult

Weather:

Temperature: _____ ° ___   Workout Gear: _____

Notes: _____

_____

_____

Vitals:

Resting HR: _____ bpm   Weight: _____ kg/lbs   Hours Slept: _____ hrs

Sport: _____ **Workout:** _____

Course: _____   Duration: _____   Distance: _____

Intensity: ☐ Max. Effort   ☐ Hard Effort   ☐ Medium Effort   ☐ Easy Effort

Average HR: _____ bpm   Target HR: _____ bpm

Feeling: ☐ Fantastic   ☐ Good   ☐ Difficult   ☐ Very Difficult

Weather:

Temperature: _____ ° ___   Workout Gear: _____

Notes: _____

_____

_____

Thursday

Vitals:

Resting HR: _____ bpm   Weight: _____ kg/lbs   Hours Slept: _____ hrs

Sport: _____ **Workout:** _____

Course: _____   Duration: _____   Distance: _____

Intensity: ☐ Max. Effort   ☐ Hard Effort   ☐ Medium Effort   ☐ Easy Effort

Average HR: _____ bpm   Target HR: _____ bpm

Feeling: ☐ Fantastic   ☐ Good   ☐ Difficult   ☐ Very Difficult

Weather:

Temperature: _____ ° ___   Workout Gear: _____

Notes: _____

_____

_____

Friday

Vitals:

Resting HR: _____ bpm   Weight: _____ kg/lbs   Hours Slept: _____ hrs

Sport: _____ **Workout:** _____

Course: _____   Duration: _____   Distance: _____

Intensity: ☐ Max. Effort   ☐ Hard Effort   ☐ Medium Effort   ☐ Easy Effort

Average HR: _____ bpm   Target HR: _____ bpm

Feeling: ☐ Fantastic   ☐ Good   ☐ Difficult   ☐ Very Difficult

Weather:

Temperature: _____ ° ___   Workout Gear: _____

Notes: _____

_____

_____

Vitals:

Resting HR: _____ bpm   Weight: _____ kg/lbs   Hours Slept: _____ hrs

Sport: _____   **Workout:** _____

Course: _____   Duration: _____   Distance: _____

Intensity: ☐ Max. Effort   ☐ Hard Effort   ☐ Medium Effort   ☐ Easy Effort

Average HR: _____ bpm   Target HR: _____ bpm

Feeling: ☐ Fantastic   ☐ Good   ☐ Difficult   ☐ Very Difficult

Weather:

Temperature: _____ ° ___   Workout Gear: _____

Notes: _____

_____

_____

Week Summary

Distance / Time (y-axis)

Sunday   Monday   Tuesday   Wednesday   Thursday   Friday   Saturday

Day

Total Time: _____ Total Distance: _____

Additional Notes: _____

_____

_____

_____

_____

_____

"You can't be lackadaisical in training and concentrate in a meet."

—Edwin Moses

Vitals:

Resting HR: _____ bpm   Weight: _____ kg/lbs   Hours Slept: _____ hrs

Sport: _____   **Workout:** _____

Course: _____   Duration: _____   Distance: _____

Intensity: ☐ Max. Effort   ☐ Hard Effort   ☐ Medium Effort   ☐ Easy Effort

Average HR: _____ bpm   Target HR: _____ bpm

Feeling: ☐ Fantastic   ☐ Good   ☐ Difficult   ☐ Very Difficult

Weather:

Temperature: _____ ° ___   Workout Gear: _____

Notes: _____

_____

_____

Vitals:

Resting HR: _____ bpm   Weight: _____ kg/lbs   Hours Slept: _____ hrs

Sport: _____   **Workout:** _____

Course: _____   Duration: _____   Distance: _____

Intensity: ☐ Max. Effort   ☐ Hard Effort   ☐ Medium Effort   ☐ Easy Effort

Average HR: _____ bpm   Target HR: _____ bpm

Feeling: ☐ Fantastic   ☐ Good   ☐ Difficult   ☐ Very Difficult

Weather:

Temperature: _____ ° ___   Workout Gear: _____

Notes: _____

_____

_____

Vitals:

Resting HR: _____ bpm   Weight: _____ kg/lbs   Hours Slept: _____ hrs

Sport: _____   **Workout:** _____

Course: _____   Duration: _____   Distance: _____

Intensity: ☐ Max. Effort   ☐ Hard Effort   ☐ Medium Effort   ☐ Easy Effort

Average HR: _____ bpm   Target HR: _____ bpm

Feeling: ☐ Fantastic   ☐ Good   ☐ Difficult   ☐ Very Difficult

Weather:

Temperature: _____ ° ___   Workout Gear: _____

Notes: _____

_____

_____

Vitals:

Resting HR: _____ bpm   Weight: _____ kg/lbs   Hours Slept: _____ hrs

Sport: _____   **Workout:** _____

Course: _____   Duration: _____   Distance: _____

Intensity: □ Max. Effort   □ Hard Effort   □ Medium Effort   □ Easy Effort

Average HR: _____ bpm   Target HR: _____ bpm

Feeling: □ Fantastic   □ Good   □ Difficult   □ Very Difficult

Weather:

Temperature: _____ ° ___   Workout Gear: _____

Notes: _____
_____
_____

Thursday

Vitals:

Resting HR: _____ bpm   Weight: _____ kg/lbs   Hours Slept: _____ hrs

Sport: _____   **Workout:** _____

Course: _____   Duration: _____   Distance: _____

Intensity: □ Max. Effort   □ Hard Effort   □ Medium Effort   □ Easy Effort

Average HR: _____ bpm   Target HR: _____ bpm

Feeling: □ Fantastic   □ Good   □ Difficult   □ Very Difficult

Weather:

Temperature: _____ ° ___   Workout Gear: _____

Notes: _____
_____
_____

Friday

Vitals:

Resting HR: _____ bpm   Weight: _____ kg/lbs   Hours Slept: _____ hrs

Sport: _____   **Workout:** _____

Course: _____   Duration: _____   Distance: _____

Intensity: □ Max. Effort   □ Hard Effort   □ Medium Effort   □ Easy Effort

Average HR: _____ bpm   Target HR: _____ bpm

Feeling: □ Fantastic   □ Good   □ Difficult   □ Very Difficult

Weather:

Temperature: _____ ° ___   Workout Gear: _____

Notes: _____
_____
_____

Vitals:

Resting HR: _____ bpm   Weight: _____ kg/lbs   Hours Slept: _____ hrs

Sport: _____   **Workout:** _____

Course: _____   Duration: _____   Distance: _____

Intensity: ☐ Max. Effort   ☐ Hard Effort   ☐ Medium Effort   ☐ Easy Effort

Average HR: _____ bpm   Target HR: _____ bpm

Feeling: ☐ Fantastic   ☐ Good   ☐ Difficult   ☐ Very Difficult

Weather:

Temperature: _____ ° ___   Workout Gear: _____

Notes: _____

_____

_____

Week Summary

Total Time: _____ Total Distance: _____

Additional Notes: _____ _____

_____

_____

_____

_____

_____

"IF YOU WANT TO BECOME THE
BEST RUNNER YOU CAN BE, START
NOW. DON'T SPEND THE REST OF
YOUR LIFE WONDERING IF YOU
CAN DO IT."

— PRISCIALLA WELCH, OLYMPIAN
& NYC MARATHON WINNER

Vitals:

Resting HR: _____ bpm　Weight: _____ kg/lbs　Hours Slept: _____ hrs

Sport: _____　**Workout:** _____

Course: _____　Duration: _____　Distance: _____

Intensity:　☐ Max. Effort　☐ Hard Effort　☐ Medium Effort　☐ Easy Effort

Average HR: _____ bpm　Target HR: _____ bpm

Feeling:　☐ Fantastic　☐ Good　☐ Difficult　☐ Very Difficult

Weather:

Temperature: _____ ° ___　Workout Gear: _____

Notes: _____

_____

_____

Monday

Vitals:

Resting HR: _____ bpm　Weight: _____ kg/lbs　Hours Slept: _____ hrs

Sport: _____　**Workout:** _____

Course: _____　Duration: _____　Distance: _____

Intensity:　☐ Max. Effort　☐ Hard Effort　☐ Medium Effort　☐ Easy Effort

Average HR: _____ bpm　Target HR: _____ bpm

Feeling:　☐ Fantastic　☐ Good　☐ Difficult　☐ Very Difficult

Weather:

Temperature: _____ ° ___　Workout Gear: _____

Notes: _____

_____

_____

Tuesday

Vitals:

Resting HR: _____ bpm　Weight: _____ kg/lbs　Hours Slept: _____ hrs

Sport: _____　**Workout:** _____

Course: _____　Duration: _____　Distance: _____

Intensity:　☐ Max. Effort　☐ Hard Effort　☐ Medium Effort　☐ Easy Effort

Average HR: _____ bpm　Target HR: _____ bpm

Feeling:　☐ Fantastic　☐ Good　☐ Difficult　☐ Very Difficult

Weather:

Temperature: _____ ° ___　Workout Gear: _____

Notes: _____

_____

_____

Vitals:

Resting HR: _____ bpm   Weight: _____ kg/lbs   Hours Slept: _____ hrs

Sport: _____   Workout: _____

Course: _____   Duration: _____   Distance: _____

Intensity: ☐ Max. Effort   ☐ Hard Effort   ☐ Medium Effort   ☐ Easy Effort

Average HR: _____ bpm   Target HR: _____ bpm

Feeling: ☐ Fantastic   ☐ Good   ☐ Difficult   ☐ Very Difficult

Weather:

Temperature: _____ ° ___   Workout Gear: _____

Notes: _____
_____
_____

Thursday

Vitals:

Resting HR: _____ bpm   Weight: _____ kg/lbs   Hours Slept: _____ hrs

Sport: _____   Workout: _____

Course: _____   Duration: _____   Distance: _____

Intensity: ☐ Max. Effort   ☐ Hard Effort   ☐ Medium Effort   ☐ Easy Effort

Average HR: _____ bpm   Target HR: _____ bpm

Feeling: ☐ Fantastic   ☐ Good   ☐ Difficult   ☐ Very Difficult

Weather:

Temperature: _____ ° ___   Workout Gear: _____

Notes: _____
_____
_____

Friday

Vitals:

Resting HR: _____ bpm   Weight: _____ kg/lbs   Hours Slept: _____ hrs

Sport: _____   Workout: _____

Course: _____   Duration: _____   Distance: _____

Intensity: ☐ Max. Effort   ☐ Hard Effort   ☐ Medium Effort   ☐ Easy Effort

Average HR: _____ bpm   Target HR: _____ bpm

Feeling: ☐ Fantastic   ☐ Good   ☐ Difficult   ☐ Very Difficult

Weather:

Temperature: _____ ° ___   Workout Gear: _____

Notes: _____
_____
_____

Vitals:

Resting HR: _____ bpm   Weight: _____ kg/lbs   Hours Slept: _____ hrs

Sport: _____   **Workout:** _____

Course: _____   Duration: _____   Distance: _____

Intensity: ☐ Max. Effort   ☐ Hard Effort   ☐ Medium Effort   ☐ Easy Effort

Average HR: _____ bpm   Target HR: _____ bpm

Feeling: ☐ Fantastic   ☐ Good   ☐ Difficult   ☐ Very Difficult

Weather:

Temperature: _____ ° ___   Workout Gear: _____

Notes: _____
_____
_____

Week Summary

Total Time: _____ Total Distance: _____

Additional Notes: _____
_____
_____
_____
_____
_____

"MENTAL WILL IS A MUSCLE THAT NEEDS EXERCISE, JUST LIKE MUSCLES OF THE BODY." — LYNN JENNINGS

Vitals:
Resting HR: _____ bpm   Weight: _____ kg/lbs   Hours Slept: _____ hrs

Sport: _____   **Workout:** _____

Course: _____   Duration: _____   Distance: _____

Intensity: ☐ Max. Effort   ☐ Hard Effort   ☐ Medium Effort   ☐ Easy Effort

Average HR: _____ bpm   Target HR: _____ bpm

Feeling: ☐ Fantastic   ☐ Good   ☐ Difficult   ☐ Very Difficult

Weather:
Temperature: _____ ° ___   Workout Gear: _____

Notes: _____

_____

_____

Vitals:
Resting HR: _____ bpm   Weight: _____ kg/lbs   Hours Slept: _____ hrs

Sport: _____   **Workout:** _____

Course: _____   Duration: _____   Distance: _____

Intensity: ☐ Max. Effort   ☐ Hard Effort   ☐ Medium Effort   ☐ Easy Effort

Average HR: _____ bpm   Target HR: _____ bpm

Feeling: ☐ Fantastic   ☐ Good   ☐ Difficult   ☐ Very Difficult

Weather:
Temperature: _____ ° ___   Workout Gear: _____

Notes: _____

_____

_____

Vitals:
Resting HR: _____ bpm   Weight: _____ kg/lbs   Hours Slept: _____ hrs

Sport: _____   **Workout:** _____

Course: _____   Duration: _____   Distance: _____

Intensity: ☐ Max. Effort   ☐ Hard Effort   ☐ Medium Effort   ☐ Easy Effort

Average HR: _____ bpm   Target HR: _____ bpm

Feeling: ☐ Fantastic   ☐ Good   ☐ Difficult   ☐ Very Difficult

Weather:
Temperature: _____ ° ___   Workout Gear: _____

Notes: _____

_____

_____

Vitals:

Resting HR: _____ bpm   Weight: _____ kg/lbs   Hours Slept: _____ hrs

Sport: _____   **Workout:** _____

Course: _____   Duration: _____   Distance: _____

Intensity: ☐ Max. Effort   ☐ Hard Effort   ☐ Medium Effort   ☐ Easy Effort

Average HR: _____ bpm   Target HR: _____ bpm

Feeling: ☐ Fantastic   ☐ Good   ☐ Difficult   ☐ Very Difficult

Weather:

Temperature: _____ ° ___   Workout Gear: _____

Notes: _____
_____
_____

Vitals:

Resting HR: _____ bpm   Weight: _____ kg/lbs   Hours Slept: _____ hrs

Sport: _____   **Workout:** _____

Course: _____   Duration: _____   Distance: _____

Intensity: ☐ Max. Effort   ☐ Hard Effort   ☐ Medium Effort   ☐ Easy Effort

Average HR: _____ bpm   Target HR: _____ bpm

Feeling: ☐ Fantastic   ☐ Good   ☐ Difficult   ☐ Very Difficult

Weather:

Temperature: _____ ° ___   Workout Gear: _____

Notes: _____
_____
_____

Vitals:

Resting HR: _____ bpm   Weight: _____ kg/lbs   Hours Slept: _____ hrs

Sport: _____   **Workout:** _____

Course: _____   Duration: _____   Distance: _____

Intensity: ☐ Max. Effort   ☐ Hard Effort   ☐ Medium Effort   ☐ Easy Effort

Average HR: _____ bpm   Target HR: _____ bpm

Feeling: ☐ Fantastic   ☐ Good   ☐ Difficult   ☐ Very Difficult

Weather:

Temperature: _____ ° ___   Workout Gear: _____

Notes: _____
_____
_____

Vitals:

Resting HR: _____ bpm   Weight: _____ kg/lbs   Hours Slept: _____ hrs

Sport: _____   **Workout:** _____

Course: _____   Duration: _____   Distance: _____

Intensity: ☐ Max. Effort   ☐ Hard Effort   ☐ Medium Effort   ☐ Easy Effort

Average HR: _____ bpm   Target HR: _____ bpm

Feeling: ☐ Fantastic   ☐ Good   ☐ Difficult   ☐ Very Difficult

Weather:

Temperature: _____ ° ___   Workout Gear: _____

Notes: _____

_____

_____

Week Summary

Distance / Time

	Sunday	Monday	Tuesday	Wednesday	Thursday	Friday	Saturday

Day

Total Time: _____ Total Distance: _____

Additional Notes: _____

_____

_____

_____

_____

"Running is a big question mark that's there each and every day. It asks you, 'Are you going to be a wimp or are you going to be strong today?'"

— Peter Maher,
Irish-Canadian
Olympian and
sub-2:12 marathoner

Vitals:

Resting HR: _____ bpm   Weight: _____ kg/lbs   Hours Slept: _____ hrs

Sport: _____ **Workout:** _____

Course: _____   Duration: _____   Distance: _____

Intensity: ☐ Max. Effort ☐ Hard Effort ☐ Medium Effort ☐ Easy Effort

Average HR: _____ bpm   Target HR: _____ bpm

Feeling: ☐ Fantastic   ☐ Good   ☐ Difficult   ☐ Very Difficult

Weather:

Temperature: _____°___   Workout Gear: _____

Notes: _____
_____
_____

Monday

Vitals:

Resting HR: _____ bpm   Weight: _____ kg/lbs   Hours Slept: _____ hrs

Sport: _____ **Workout:** _____

Course: _____   Duration: _____   Distance: _____

Intensity: ☐ Max. Effort ☐ Hard Effort ☐ Medium Effort ☐ Easy Effort

Average HR: _____ bpm   Target HR: _____ bpm

Feeling: ☐ Fantastic   ☐ Good   ☐ Difficult   ☐ Very Difficult

Weather:

Temperature: _____°___   Workout Gear: _____

Notes: _____
_____
_____

Tuesday

Vitals:

Resting HR: _____ bpm   Weight: _____ kg/lbs   Hours Slept: _____ hrs

Sport: _____ **Workout:** _____

Course: _____   Duration: _____   Distance: _____

Intensity: ☐ Max. Effort ☐ Hard Effort ☐ Medium Effort ☐ Easy Effort

Average HR: _____ bpm   Target HR: _____ bpm

Feeling: ☐ Fantastic   ☐ Good   ☐ Difficult   ☐ Very Difficult

Weather:

Temperature: _____°___   Workout Gear: _____

Notes: _____
_____
_____

Wednesday   Week 49

Vitals:

Resting HR: _____ bpm   Weight: _____ kg/lbs   Hours Slept: _____ hrs

Sport: _____ **Workout:** _____

Course: _____ Duration: _____ Distance: _____

Intensity: ☐ Max. Effort ☐ Hard Effort   ☐ Medium Effort   ☐ Easy Effort

Average HR: _____ bpm   Target HR: _____ bpm

Feeling: ☐ Fantastic   ☐ Good   ☐ Difficult   ☐ Very Difficult

Weather:

Temperature: _____ °___   Workout Gear: _____

Notes: _____
_____
_____

Thursday

Vitals:

Resting HR: _____ bpm   Weight: _____ kg/lbs   Hours Slept: _____ hrs

Sport: _____ **Workout:** _____

Course: _____ Duration: _____ Distance: _____

Intensity: ☐ Max. Effort ☐ Hard Effort   ☐ Medium Effort   ☐ Easy Effort

Average HR: _____ bpm   Target HR: _____ bpm

Feeling: ☐ Fantastic   ☐ Good   ☐ Difficult   ☐ Very Difficult

Weather:

Temperature: _____ °___   Workout Gear: _____

Notes: _____
_____
_____

Friday

Vitals:

Resting HR: _____ bpm   Weight: _____ kg/lbs   Hours Slept: _____ hrs

Sport: _____ **Workout:** _____

Course: _____ Duration: _____ Distance: _____

Intensity: ☐ Max. Effort ☐ Hard Effort   ☐ Medium Effort   ☐ Easy Effort

Average HR: _____ bpm   Target HR: _____ bpm

Feeling: ☐ Fantastic   ☐ Good   ☐ Difficult   ☐ Very Difficult

Weather:

Temperature: _____ °___   Workout Gear: _____

Notes: _____
_____
_____

Week 49　　Date: ▮ ▮ ▮　　Saturday

Vitals:

Resting HR: _____ bpm　　Weight: _____ kg/lbs　Hours Slept: _____ hrs

Sport: _____　**Workout:** _____

Course: _____　Duration: _____　Distance: _____

Intensity:　☐ Max. Effort　☐ Hard Effort　☐ Medium Effort　☐ Easy Effort

Average HR: _____ bpm　　Target HR: _____ bpm

Feeling:　☐ Fantastic　☐ Good　☐ Difficult　☐ Very Difficult

Weather:

Temperature: _____ ° ___　Workout Gear: _____

Notes: _____

_____

_____

Week Summary

Distance / Time

Sunday　Monday　Tuesday　Wednesday　Thursday　Friday　Saturday

Day

Total Time: _____　Total Distance: _____

Additional Notes: _____

_____

_____

_____

_____

_____

"The man who can drive himself further once the effort gets painful is the man who will win." — Roger Bannister, first 4 min miler

Vitals:

Resting HR: _____ bpm   Weight: _____ kg/lbs   Hours Slept: _____ hrs

Sport: _____   **Workout:** _____

Course: _____   Duration: _____   Distance: _____

Intensity: ☐ Max. Effort   ☐ Hard Effort   ☐ Medium Effort   ☐ Easy Effort

Average HR: _____ bpm   Target HR: _____ bpm

Feeling: ☐ Fantastic   ☐ Good   ☐ Difficult   ☐ Very Difficult

Weather:

Temperature: _____ ° ___   Workout Gear: _____

Notes: _____

_____

_____

Vitals:

Resting HR: _____ bpm   Weight: _____ kg/lbs   Hours Slept: _____ hrs

Sport: _____   **Workout:** _____

Course: _____   Duration: _____   Distance: _____

Intensity: ☐ Max. Effort   ☐ Hard Effort   ☐ Medium Effort   ☐ Easy Effort

Average HR: _____ bpm   Target HR: _____ bpm

Feeling: ☐ Fantastic   ☐ Good   ☐ Difficult   ☐ Very Difficult

Weather:

Temperature: _____ ° ___   Workout Gear: _____

Notes: _____

_____

_____

Vitals:

Resting HR: _____ bpm   Weight: _____ kg/lbs   Hours Slept: _____ hrs

Sport: _____   **Workout:** _____

Course: _____   Duration: _____   Distance: _____

Intensity: ☐ Max. Effort   ☐ Hard Effort   ☐ Medium Effort   ☐ Easy Effort

Average HR: _____ bpm   Target HR: _____ bpm

Feeling: ☐ Fantastic   ☐ Good   ☐ Difficult   ☐ Very Difficult

Weather:

Temperature: _____ ° ___   Workout Gear: _____

Notes: _____

_____

_____

Vitals:

Resting HR: _____ bpm   Weight: _____ kg/lbs   Hours Slept: _____ hrs

Sport: _____   **Workout:** _____

Course: _____   Duration: _____   Distance: _____

Intensity: ☐ Max. Effort   ☐ Hard Effort   ☐ Medium Effort   ☐ Easy Effort

Average HR: _____ bpm   Target HR: _____ bpm

Feeling: ☐ Fantastic   ☐ Good   ☐ Difficult   ☐ Very Difficult

Weather:

Temperature: _____ ° ___   Workout Gear: _____

Notes: _____
_____
_____

Thursday

Vitals:

Resting HR: _____ bpm   Weight: _____ kg/lbs   Hours Slept: _____ hrs

Sport: _____   **Workout:** _____

Course: _____   Duration: _____   Distance: _____

Intensity: ☐ Max. Effort   ☐ Hard Effort   ☐ Medium Effort   ☐ Easy Effort

Average HR: _____ bpm   Target HR: _____ bpm

Feeling: ☐ Fantastic   ☐ Good   ☐ Difficult   ☐ Very Difficult

Weather:

Temperature: _____ ° ___   Workout Gear: _____

Notes: _____
_____
_____

Friday

Vitals:

Resting HR: _____ bpm   Weight: _____ kg/lbs   Hours Slept: _____ hrs

Sport: _____   **Workout:** _____

Course: _____   Duration: _____   Distance: _____

Intensity: ☐ Max. Effort   ☐ Hard Effort   ☐ Medium Effort   ☐ Easy Effort

Average HR: _____ bpm   Target HR: _____ bpm

Feeling: ☐ Fantastic   ☐ Good   ☐ Difficult   ☐ Very Difficult

Weather:

Temperature: _____ ° ___   Workout Gear: _____

Notes: _____
_____
_____

Vitals:

Resting HR: _____ bpm   Weight: _____ kg/lbs   Hours Slept: _____ hrs

Sport: _____   **Workout:** _____

Course: _____   Duration: _____   Distance: _____

Intensity: ☐ Max. Effort   ☐ Hard Effort   ☐ Medium Effort   ☐ Easy Effort

Average HR: _____ bpm   Target HR: _____ bpm

Feeling: ☐ Fantastic   ☐ Good   ☐ Difficult   ☐ Very Difficult

Weather:

Temperature: _____ ° ___   Workout Gear: _____

Notes: _____
_____
_____

Week Summary

Day

Total Time: _____ Total Distance: _____

Additional Notes: _____
_____
_____
_____
_____
_____

"When you have to make a choice and don't make it, that is in itself a choice."
— William James

Week 51   Date: ☐ ☐ ☐   Sunday

Vitals:

Resting HR: _____ bpm   Weight: _____ kg/lbs   Hours Slept: _____ hrs

Sport: _____   **Workout:** _____

Course: _____   Duration: _____   Distance: _____

Intensity: ☐ Max. Effort   ☐ Hard Effort   ☐ Medium Effort   ☐ Easy Effort

Average HR: _____ bpm   Target HR: _____ bpm

Feeling: ☐ Fantastic   ☐ Good   ☐ Difficult   ☐ Very Difficult

Weather:

Temperature: _____°___   Workout Gear: _____

Notes: _____

_____

_____

Monday

Vitals:

Resting HR: _____ bpm   Weight: _____ kg/lbs   Hours Slept: _____ hrs

Sport: _____   **Workout:** _____

Course: _____   Duration: _____   Distance: _____

Intensity: ☐ Max. Effort   ☐ Hard Effort   ☐ Medium Effort   ☐ Easy Effort

Average HR: _____ bpm   Target HR: _____ bpm

Feeling: ☐ Fantastic   ☐ Good   ☐ Difficult   ☐ Very Difficult

Weather:

Temperature: _____°___   Workout Gear: _____

Notes: _____

_____

_____

Tuesday

Vitals:

Resting HR: _____ bpm   Weight: _____ kg/lbs   Hours Slept: _____ hrs

Sport: _____   **Workout:** _____

Course: _____   Duration: _____   Distance: _____

Intensity: ☐ Max. Effort   ☐ Hard Effort   ☐ Medium Effort   ☐ Easy Effort

Average HR: _____ bpm   Target HR: _____ bpm

Feeling: ☐ Fantastic   ☐ Good   ☐ Difficult   ☐ Very Difficult

Weather:

Temperature: _____°___   Workout Gear: _____

Notes: _____

_____

_____

Wednesday Week 51

Vitals:

Resting HR: _____ bpm   Weight: _____ kg/lbs   Hours Slept: _____ hrs

Sport: _____ **Workout:** _____

Course: _____   Duration: _____   Distance: _____

Intensity: ☐ Max. Effort   ☐ Hard Effort   ☐ Medium Effort   ☐ Easy Effort

Average HR: _____ bpm   Target HR: _____ bpm

Feeling: ☐ Fantastic   ☐ Good   ☐ Difficult   ☐ Very Difficult

Weather:

Temperature: _____ ° __   Workout Gear: _____

Notes: _____
_____
_____

Thursday

Vitals:

Resting HR: _____ bpm   Weight: _____ kg/lbs   Hours Slept: _____ hrs

Sport: _____ **Workout:** _____

Course: _____   Duration: _____   Distance: _____

Intensity: ☐ Max. Effort   ☐ Hard Effort   ☐ Medium Effort   ☐ Easy Effort

Average HR: _____ bpm   Target HR: _____ bpm

Feeling: ☐ Fantastic   ☐ Good   ☐ Difficult   ☐ Very Difficult

Weather:

Temperature: _____ ° __   Workout Gear: _____

Notes: _____
_____
_____

Friday

Vitals:

Resting HR: _____ bpm   Weight: _____ kg/lbs   Hours Slept: _____ hrs

Sport: _____ **Workout:** _____

Course: _____   Duration: _____   Distance: _____

Intensity: ☐ Max. Effort   ☐ Hard Effort   ☐ Medium Effort   ☐ Easy Effort

Average HR: _____ bpm   Target HR: _____ bpm

Feeling: ☐ Fantastic   ☐ Good   ☐ Difficult   ☐ Very Difficult

Weather:

Temperature: _____ ° __   Workout Gear: _____ _____

Notes: _____
_____
_____

Vitals:

Resting HR: _____ bpm   Weight: _____ kg/lbs   Hours Slept: _____ hrs

Sport: _____   **Workout:** _____

Course: _____   Duration: _____   Distance: _____

Intensity: ☐ Max. Effort   ☐ Hard Effort   ☐ Medium Effort   ☐ Easy Effort

Average HR: _____ bpm   Target HR: _____ bpm

Feeling: ☐ Fantastic   ☐ Good   ☐ Difficult   ☐ Very Difficult

Weather:

Temperature: _____ ° ___   Workout Gear: _____

Notes: _____

_____

_____

Week Summary

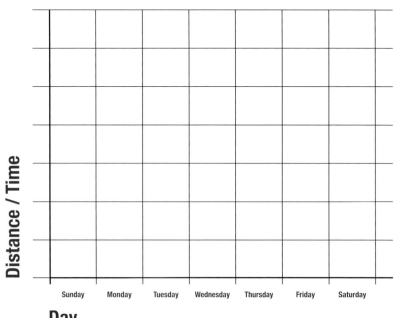

Day

Total Time: _____ Total Distance: _____

Additional Notes: _____

_____

_____

_____

_____

_____

Vitals:

Resting HR: _____ bpm　　Weight: _____ kg/lbs　Hours Slept: _____ hrs

Sport: _____　**Workout:** _____

Course: _____　　Duration: _____　　Distance: _____

Intensity:　☐ Max. Effort　☐ Hard Effort　☐ Medium Effort　☐ Easy Effort

Average HR: _____ bpm　　Target HR: _____ bpm

Feeling:　☐ Fantastic　☐ Good　☐ Difficult　☐ Very Difficult

Weather:

Temperature: _____ ° ___　　Workout Gear: _____

Notes: _____

_____

_____

Monday

Vitals:

Resting HR: _____ bpm　　Weight: _____ kg/lbs　Hours Slept: _____ hrs

Sport: _____　**Workout:** _____

Course: _____　　Duration: _____　　Distance: _____

Intensity:　☐ Max. Effort　☐ Hard Effort　☐ Medium Effort　☐ Easy Effort

Average HR: _____ bpm　　Target HR: _____ bpm

Feeling:　☐ Fantastic　☐ Good　☐ Difficult　☐ Very Difficult

Weather:

Temperature: _____ ° ___　　Workout Gear: _____

Notes: _____

_____

_____

Tuesday

Vitals:

Resting HR: _____ bpm　　Weight: _____ kg/lbs　Hours Slept: _____ hrs

Sport: _____　**Workout:** _____

Course: _____　　Duration: _____　　Distance: _____

Intensity:　☐ Max. Effort　☐ Hard Effort　☐ Medium Effort　☐ Easy Effort

Average HR: _____ bpm　　Target HR: _____ bpm

Feeling:　☐ Fantastic　☐ Good　☐ Difficult　☐ Very Difficult

Weather:

Temperature: _____ ° ___　　Workout Gear: _____

Notes: _____

_____

_____

Vitals:

Resting HR: _____ bpm   Weight: _____ kg/lbs   Hours Slept: _____ hrs

Sport: _____ **Workout:** _____

Course: _____   Duration: _____   Distance: _____

Intensity: ☐ Max. Effort   ☐ Hard Effort   ☐ Medium Effort   ☐ Easy Effort

Average HR: _____ bpm   Target HR: _____ bpm

Feeling: ☐ Fantastic   ☐ Good   ☐ Difficult   ☐ Very Difficult

Weather:

Temperature: _____ ° ___   Workout Gear: _____

Notes: _____
_____
_____

Thursday

Vitals:

Resting HR: _____ bpm   Weight: _____ kg/lbs   Hours Slept: _____ hrs

Sport: _____ **Workout:** _____

Course: _____   Duration: _____   Distance: _____

Intensity: ☐ Max. Effort   ☐ Hard Effort   ☐ Medium Effort   ☐ Easy Effort

Average HR: _____ bpm   Target HR: _____ bpm

Feeling: ☐ Fantastic   ☐ Good   ☐ Difficult   ☐ Very Difficult

Weather:

Temperature: _____ ° ___   Workout Gear: _____

Notes: _____
_____
_____

Friday

Vitals:

Resting HR: _____ bpm   Weight: _____ kg/lbs   Hours Slept: _____ hrs

Sport: _____ **Workout:** _____

Course: _____   Duration: _____   Distance: _____

Intensity: ☐ Max. Effort   ☐ Hard Effort   ☐ Medium Effort   ☐ Easy Effort

Average HR: _____ bpm   Target HR: _____ bpm

Feeling: ☐ Fantastic   ☐ Good   ☐ Difficult   ☐ Very Difficult

Weather:

Temperature: _____ ° ___   Workout Gear: _____

Notes: _____
_____
_____

Vitals:

Resting HR: _____ bpm   Weight: _____ kg/lbs   Hours Slept: _____ hrs

Sport: _____   **Workout:** _____

Course: _____   Duration: _____   Distance: _____

Intensity: ☐ Max. Effort   ☐ Hard Effort   ☐ Medium Effort   ☐ Easy Effort

Average HR: _____ bpm   Target HR: _____ bpm

Feeling: ☐ Fantastic   ☐ Good   ☐ Difficult   ☐ Very Difficult

Weather:

Temperature: _____ ° ___   Workout Gear: _____

Notes: _____

_____

_____

Week Summary

Total Time: _____ Total Distance: _____

Additional Notes: _____

_____

_____

_____

_____

_____

42 KM

Running Room LTD

"The greater the obstacle, the more glory in overcoming it."
— Moliere

Race Records

Date	Name/Location	Distance	Time	Pace

Date	Name/Location	Distance	Time	Pace

Index